AN A

MW01028113

Julius Caesar

William Shakespeare

GLOBE FEARON
EDUCATIONAL PUBLISHER

A Division of Simon & Schuster
Upper Saddle River, New Jersey

Adapter: Mark Falstein
Project Editor: Kristen Shepos-Salvatore
Editorial Supervisor: Cary Pepper
Editorial Assistant: Kathleen Kennedy
Production Editor: Alan Dalgleish
Marketing Manager: Sandra Hutchison
Art Supervision: Patricia Smythe
Electronic Page Production: Luc VanMeerbeek
Cover and Interior Illustrator: James McDaniel

Printed in the United States of America.
3 4 5 6 7 8 9 10 04 03 02 01 00

ISBN: 0-835-91847-5

GLOBE FEARON EDUCATIONAL PUBLISHER
Upper Saddle River, New Jersey
www.globefearon.com

CONTENTS

ABOUT THE AUTHOR

There are many things we do not know for certain about William Shakespeare. It is believed he was born on April 26, 1564. He grew up in Stratford upon Avon, a small town in England. He married Anne Hathaway in 1582, when he was 18. They had three children, two girls and one boy. Shakespeare went to London, where he became successful as an actor, a playwright, and a poet. He belonged to a group of actors called The King's Men, who performed his plays. In 1599, The King's Men built a theater, which they named the Globe. The Globe became one of the best-known theaters in London. Shakespeare's plays were also performed at court, for Queen Elizabeth I and King James I. Shakespeare retired from the theater around 1613. He returned to Stratford, where he bought a house and land. William Shakespeare died on April 23, 1616. He is buried in Stratford.

Who really wrote Shakespeare's plays is one of literature's great mysteries. Some people say that one man could not have written so many excellent plays. Some people think that if one man did write them, it was not Shakespeare, because they believe he was poorly educated. Other people say he did write the plays that bear his name, and consider William Shakespeare the world's greatest playwright.

ADAPTER'S NOTE

In preparing this edition of *Julius Caesar,* we have kept closely to Shakespeare's words and thoughts. We have changed some vocabulary and simplified many sentences. Many words and phrases that were common 400 years ago are poorly understood today. We have expressed these in clear, modern English. In places where we have changed the language, we have preserved the sense of Shakespeare's poetic images. The most famous lines have been kept as Shakespeare wrote them.

PREFACE

Julius Caesar was first performed in about 1599. At that time, many people in England were interested in the ancient Romans. A key event in Roman history was the murder of Julius Caesar in 44 B.C. Caesar was a Roman general and a powerful ruler. His killers were led by Marcus Brutus, Caesar's best friend.

Shakespeare's audiences knew this story well but often had different views about the characters. Was Caesar a "man of the people"? Or was he a tyrant who threatened Rome's freedom? Was Brutus a traitor and a murderer? Or was he a man of honor who did what he thought was right? It is around these questions that Shakespeare built his play.

Julius Caesar is known as a "character play." The characters are true-to-life people. Caesar's killers each have their own reasons for wanting him dead. Mark Antony, Caesar's ally, uses the murder for his own ends. The only two women in the play stand out as individuals, too. They are Calpurnia and Portia, the wives of Caesar and Brutus. They have different feelings about the dangers their husbands face and about their position in the "man's world" that was ancient Rome.

Julius Caesar is one of Shakespeare's most often-performed plays. Today's audiences can easily appreciate the ideas the play raises about power, honor, and loyalty. In the 1950s, a film of the play was made featuring major Hollywood stars.

HISTORICAL BACKGROUND

History tells us that the Roman Empire fell in the year A.D. 476. But in many ways, the Roman world is still with us today. Roman roads and buildings still stand in Europe, Africa, and Asia. All or part of more than 30 present-day countries were once ruled by Rome. Places in these countries still have names the Romans gave them. English and many other languages use the Roman alphabet. The laws of many countries are based on Roman laws. The people who wrote the United States Constitution respected the ancient Romans. Rome had once been a republic, like the United States. Its rulers and lawmakers were elected by the citizens.

The Roman Republic lasted nearly 500 years. But by 27 B.C., it was gone. Rome had fallen under one-man rule. The Roman Republic had become the Roman Empire. Just how this happened is the background of Shakespeare's play, *Julius Caesar*.

Little is known about Rome's early history. Legend has it that the city was founded in 752 B.C. It grew beside the Tiber river in central Italy. At first Rome was a small settlement of farmers and shepherds. It was ruled by a people called the *Etruscans* (eh-TRUS-kuhns). Under the Etruscan kings, Rome became a rich city. In 510 B.C., the Romans rose up against the Etruscans and drove them out. They declared that Rome would never again be ruled by a king.

The Republic took shape over many years. At first only the noble families, or *patricians* (puh-TRISH-uhns), had rights. A senate, made up of patricians, made the laws. But by 287 B.C., the common people, or *plebeians* (pluh-BEE-uhns), won the rights to vote and to hold public office. Elected officials carried out the laws made by the senators and, later, by the plebeians. The leading official was called a consul. He was elected for a term of one year. There were always two consuls at any time. Neither could act unless the other agreed.

All Roman citizens had to serve in the army. At first, it was a defensive army. But during the 300s B.C., the Romans began to conquer other peoples. Between 264 and 146 B.C., they fought and won three wars against Carthage, a powerful state in Africa. These victories made Rome the leading power in its part of the world. Over the next 100 years, the Romans added to their empire.

Meanwhile, there was trouble in Rome. Rich Romans grew richer from slaves, property, and taxes taken from conquered peoples. But the poor grew poorer. Many poor farmers lost their land. There was fighting between rich and poor. Elected leaders who tried to help the poor were murdered by senators. Wars and rebellions also weakened the republic. Romans began to elect consuls for their skills at winning battles and keeping order. One consul, Gaius Marius, was well liked by the plebeians. He was elected seven times. This broke the rule that consuls could serve only one year. Marius's rival, Lucius Sulla, went even further. He was supported by the patricians. He defeated Marius and was given the title of dictator (sole ruler) in 82 B.C. He retired three years later, but for a time Romans had accepted one-man rule.

One of Sulla's generals was a man named Gaius Pompey. He had raised his own private army to help Sulla against Marius. Pompey won new territories for Rome in Asia. He returned to Rome a hero. He promised to give his soldiers land and to restore the rights that Sulla had taken from the plebeians. The senate blocked him. In 60 B.C., Pompey formed an alliance with two other men to work against the senate. One of these men was Marcus Crassus, who died a few years later. The other was a 40-year-old patrician who was popular with the plebeians. His name was Julius Caesar.

Caesar was a bright, charming man and a fine public speaker. He had been a follower of Marius, but Sulla had later pardoned him. In public life, Caesar had reached the office of praetor, one rank below consul. In 59 B.C., Pompey and his allies had Caesar elected consul. This was done mainly through threats and bribes. Caesar used his power to push through Pompey's program. This won him many enemies among the patricians in the senate. Pompey gave him the job of ruler of three provinces north of Italy.

But Caesar knew that the only way to win real power in Rome was through military conquest. The people of Gaul (modern France) had often invaded Roman territory. Caesar's provinces bordered on Gaul. This gave Caesar an excuse to invade and conquer all of Gaul. He proved himself to be a great general.

Pompey began to fear Caesar's power. He allied himself with Caesar's enemies in the senate. In 49 B.C., the senate ordered Caesar to give up his army. Caesar knew that if he did that, he would be killed. He led his army into Italy and marched on Rome. In doing so, he effectively declared war on the republic.

It took Caesar only 60 days to defeat Pompey's armies. He forced the senate to name him consul and dictator. He then led his army into Greece, to where Pompey had fled. He defeated Pompey's armies again. Pompey fled to Egypt, where he was murdered. His allies kept fighting under Pompey's sons, but Caesar defeated them in two battles.

Caesar was now master of the Roman world. There was no one to challenge him. He was named dictator for ten years. His first act was to pardon the followers of Pompey. Two men who received these pardons were Marcus Brutus and Caius Cassius.

Caesar named Brutus to two high offices. Brutus and Caesar had long been close. In fact, Roman gossip said that Brutus was really Caesar's son.

In 45 B.C., the senate and people of Rome named Caesar dictator for life. He now was a king in all but name. It is early the following year that Shakespeare's play begins.

CAST OF CHARACTERS

JULIUS CAESAR	a Roman general and statesman
CALPURNIA	his wife
Their **SERVANT**	
MARCUS BRUTUS	a noble Roman
PORTIA	his wife
LUCIUS	their servant

CAIUS CASSIUS
CASCA
CINNA
DECIUS BRUTUS
METELLUS CIMBER
TREBONIUS
CAIUS LIGARIUS
} noble Romans who, with Brutus, conspire to kill Caesar

MARK ANTONY	an officer who serves Caesar
OCTAVIUS	a general, Caesar's adopted son

CICERO
PUBLIUS
POPILIUS
LEPIDUS
FLAVIUS
MARULLUS
} noble Romans

LUCILIUS
TITINIUS
MESSALA
VARRO
CLAUDIUS
YOUNG CATO
CLITUS
DARDANUS
VOLUMNIUS
STRATO
} officers and soldiers in the armies of Brutus and Cassius

A CARPENTER
A COBBLER
A SOOTHSAYER
ARTEMIDORUS
SERVANT of Antony
SERVANT of Octavius
FIRST, SECOND, THIRD, and **FOURTH PLEBEIANS**

CINNA the Poet
PINDARUS   Cassius's slave
Another **POET**
A MESSENGER
SOLDIERS in Brutus's and Antony's armies
Citizens, Senators, Suitors, Plebeians, and Slaves

Act 1

Scene 1

A street in Rome. Two noble Romans, FLAVIUS *and* MARULLUS, *enter; also several common people, including a* CARPENTER *and a* COBBLER.

FLAVIUS: Away! You idle creatures, go on home!
　　Is this a holiday? What, don't you know?
　　Being workers, you should not be on the street
　　On this, a work day, without the sign
　　Of your profession? You, what is your job?

CARPENTER: Why, sir, I am a carpenter.

MARULLUS: Where is your leather apron and your ruler?
　　Why are you out wearing your best clothes?
　　You sir, what work do you do?

COBBLER: Work that I hope I might do, sir, with a good
　　conscience. I'm a mender of bad soles.

FLAVIUS: What job, you good-for-nothing rascal?
　　Speak!

COBBLER: Truly, sir, I'm a cobbler. All I live by is the awl.[1]
　　I'm a doctor to old shoes. When they are sick, I
　　recover them. The finest men that ever walked on
　　leather have walked upon my work.

FLAVIUS: But why aren't you in your shop today?
　　Why do you lead these men through the streets?

COBBLER: Why, to wear out their shoes. To get myself
　　more work. But truly sir, we're taking the day off to
　　see Caesar and to celebrate his victory.

---

1. **awl** tool for boring holes

MARULLUS: Why rejoice? Whom has he conquered?
What rich captives is he bringing home to Rome?
You blocks, you stones, you worse than senseless
    things!
Have you forgotten Pompey?[2] Many times
You sat upon your rooftops, in your windows,
With your children, waiting all day long
To see great Pompey ride the streets of Rome.
And when he passed, you people cheered so loud
The river Tiber trembled in her banks.
And now you put on your best clothes?
You take a holiday, throw flowers in the way
Of the man who conquered Pompey?
Be gone! Run to your houses! Beg the gods
Not to send us the plague that we deserve
For such thanklessness!

FLAVIUS: Go, good Romans. All you common people,
Go to the Tiber, and cry into the river
Until it rises to its highest point.

(*All the* COMMONERS *exit.*)

See, even the lowest of them creep away
Tongue-tied in their guilt. Go toward the Capitol.
I'll go this way. Let us strip the statues
Of their holiday scarves.

MARULLUS: May we do so?
You know it is the feast of Lupercal.[3]

FLAVIUS: It doesn't matter. Let no statues
Be hung with Caesar's trophies. I'll go around

---

2. **Pompey** a Roman general, once Caesar's ally but later his
    enemy
3. **Lupercal** a Roman religious festival held every February

And drive the common people from the streets.
You do it too, wherever you see a crowd.
These feathers, plucked from Caesar's wing,
Will make him fly at ordinary height.
Otherwise, he'd soar above us
And keep us all as terrified as slaves.

(*They exit in different directions.*)

Scene 2

The Forum in Rome. CAESAR, ANTONY, CALPURNIA, PORTIA, DECIUS, CICERO, BRUTUS, CASSIUS, CASCA, *and a* SOOTHSAYER[4] *enter; then* MARULLUS, FLAVIUS *and* CITIZENS *enter.*

CAESAR: Calpurnia—

CASCA: Quiet! Caesar speaks!

CAESAR: Calpurnia—

CALPURNIA: Here, my lord.

CAESAR: Stand in Antony's way when he runs the race.
   Antony, do not in your speed forget
   To touch Calpurnia. The old tales say
   That childless women, touched in this holy race,
   May shake off their curse and become mothers.

ANTONY: I shall remember.
   When Caesar says "Do this," it is performed.

SOOTHSAYER: Caesar!

CAESAR: Who calls?

CASCA: Everyone, be quiet!

CAESAR: Who is it in the crowd that calls to me?

---

4. **soothsayer** "truth-sayer," one who predicts the future

Speak. Caesar will hear you.

SOOTHSAYER: Beware the ides of March.[5]

CAESAR: What man is that?

BRUTUS: A soothsayer says beware the ides of March.

CAESAR: Bring him before me. Let me see his face.

CASSIUS: Fellow, come out of the crowd.

(*The* SOOTHSAYER *comes forward.*)

Look at Caesar.

CAESAR: What did you say to me? Speak again.

SOOTHSAYER: Beware the ides of March.

CAESAR: He is a dreamer. Let us leave him.

(*Trumpets sound. All but* BRUTUS *and* CASSIUS *exit.*)

CASSIUS: Will you go and watch the race with me?

BRUTUS: I don't care much for games. I do not have
The lively spirit that is in Antony.
But do not let me spoil your fun, Cassius.

CASSIUS: Brutus, I've been noticing you lately.
I have not seen in you the friendliness
You used to feel for me.

BRUTUS: Cassius, that's not it. It isn't you.
If I am troubled, it is only with myself.
Feelings have been fighting within me,
Which may have made me seem unfriendly.
I surely would not want my friends to think
That Marcus Brutus, at war with himself,
Forgets to show his love to other men.

CASSIUS: Then, friend, I have mistaken your feelings.

5. **ides of March** March 15

Because of that, I hid my thoughts from you.
Tell me, good Brutus, can you see your face?

BRUTUS: No, Cassius. The eye cannot see itself
Except by reflection in a mirror.

CASSIUS: Of course not, Brutus.
And there are those who find it very sad
That you have no such mirror that will show
Your worthiness to yourself. I have heard
That many men of great respect in Rome,
Except great Caesar, speak well of you, Brutus.
They look upon the troubles of our time
And wish you saw yourself as they see you.

BRUTUS: Into what dangers do you lead me, Cassius?
Why would you have me look into myself
For something that isn't there?

CASSIUS: Listen to me, Brutus. Since you know
You cannot see yourself but by reflection,
I will be your mirror. I am no false friend.
It's not in me to speak well to your face
And spread tales about you behind your back.
If you think I'd offer friendship at a party
To the whole crowd, then call me dangerous.

(*Loud cheering offstage.*)

BRUTUS: What is this shouting? I fear the people
Are choosing Caesar for their king.

CASSIUS: Oh, do you fear it? Then I must think
That you would not want it to happen.

BRUTUS: I would not, Cassius. Yet I love him well.
But tell me why you've kept me here so long.
What do you want to tell me?
If it's something that involves the good of Rome,

Show me honor in one eye and death in the other.
I'll look at one the same as at the other.
Let my standing with the gods depend
On whether I love honor more than I fear death.

CASSIUS: I know that you're a man of honor, Brutus.
Well, honor is what I shall talk about.
I cannot tell what you or other men
Think about life. But, speaking for myself,
I'd just as soon not live as stand in awe
Of someone who's no better than myself.
I was born as free as Caesar. So were you.
We're both as strong as he, and both of us
Can stand the winter's cold as well as he.
Once, on a cold and windy day,
He challenged me to swim across the Tiber.
Dressed as I was, I jumped right in,
And then he followed. The raging river roared,
And we fought back at it with our strong muscles,
Beating it as we tried to beat each other.
But before we reached the finish of our race,
Caesar cried, "Help me, Cassius, or I'll drown!"
I dragged him from the water on my shoulders.
And now this Caesar has become a god,
And Cassius must bend his body to him
If Caesar simply nods in his direction.
By the gods, how it amazes me that Caesar,
Weak as he is, has so outrun the world
That he alone now holds the winner's prize!

(*Loud cheering offstage.*)

BRUTUS: More shouting! I do believe they cheer
For some new honors that are given to Caesar.

CASSIUS: Why, man, he does bestride the narrow world

Like a Colossus,[6] and we petty men
Walk under his huge legs, and peep about
To find ourselves dishonorable graves!
Sometimes men are masters of their lives.
The fault, dear Brutus, is not in our stars,
But in ourselves, that we are underlings.[7]
"Brutus" and "Caesar"—what's the difference?
Why should his name count for more than yours?
Now, in the names of all the gods at once,
Upon what meat does this, our Caesar, feed
That he is grown so great? Our times are shamed!
Rome, what has happened to your great families?
When was there a time, since the great flood,
When people honored just one man alone?
When else could anyone have said of Rome
That her wide streets had room for just one man?
Oh, you and I have often heard it said
There was a Brutus once,[8] who would as soon
Have let the Devil rule Rome as any king!

BRUTUS: I have no doubt that you're my friend.
I can guess what you're asking me to do.
What I think about it, and about these times,
I'll tell you later. For now, I ask with love
That you don't speak about it any more.
I'll think about what you've said. I'll listen
Patiently to what you have to say.
We'll find a time to meet and talk about it.

---

6. **does bestride...Colossus** stands over us all like a huge statue
7. **The fault...underlings** It is the Romans' own weakness, not bad luck, that has made them servants to Caesar.
8. **There was a Brutus once** Lucius Junius Brutus, an ancestor of Marcus Brutus, led the rebellion in 510 B.C. that threw out Rome's kings and set up the Republic.

Till then, my noble friend, think about this:
Brutus would rather be a nobody
Than to call himself a son of Rome
In such times as we now live.

CASSIUS: I am glad that my weak words
Have brought forth this much fire from you, Brutus.

(CAESAR *and his followers enter.*)

BRUTUS: The games are done, and Caesar is returning.

CASSIUS: As they pass by, grab Casca's sleeve.
He will tell you, in his sour way,
If anything important happened.

BRUTUS: I will. But, Cassius, look! Caesar is angry,
And the others look like scolded children.
Calpurnia looks pale, and Cicero's eyes
Are fiery red, as when some senators
Are arguing with him.

CAESAR: Antony.

ANTONY: Caesar?

CAESAR: Let me have men about me that are fat,
Well-fed men who sleep soundly at night.
That Cassius has a lean and hungry look.
He thinks too much. Such men are dangerous.

ANTONY: Don't fear him, Caesar; he's not dangerous.
He's a noble Roman, and acts rightly.

CAESAR: I do not fear him, because I'm Caesar.
But if I were a man to be afraid,
I'd be afraid of Cassius. He reads too much.
He understands men and their thoughts too well.
He doesn't go to plays or listen to music,
As you do, Antony. He rarely smiles,

And when he does, he seems to mock himself,
As if he hates that he could smile at anything.
Such men are never happy when they see
Another man who's greater than themselves.
Therefore, such men are very dangerous.
Come on my right side, for this ear is deaf.
Now, tell me truly what you think of him.

(*Trumpets sound.* CAESAR *and his followers exit, except for* CASCA, *who stays behind.*)

CASCA: You grabbed my sleeve. You want to talk to me?

BRUTUS: Yes, Casca. Tell us what happened today
  To make Caesar look so sad.

CASCA: Why, there was a crown offered to him, and he
  pushed it away with the back of his hand, and the
  people started shouting.

CASSIUS: They shouted three times.
  Was the crown offered him three times?

CASCA: Yes, it was, and he pushed it away three times,
  and each time gentler than before; and each time my
  neighbors shouted.

CASSIUS: Who offered him the crown?

CASCA: Why, Antony.

BRUTUS: Tell us how it happened, gentle Casca.

CASCA: I can as well be hanged as say how it happened.
  It was foolishness; I paid no attention to it. Mark
  Antony offered him the crown. It wasn't a real crown,
  just a small one. As I told you, he pushed it away.
  But if you ask me, I think he wanted to take it. Then
  Antony offered it to him again, and he pushed it
  away again. But it looked to me like he hated to take

his fingers off it. And then he was offered it the third time. He pushed it away again, and the common people hooted and clapped their hands and threw up their sweaty caps because Caesar refused the crown. I tell you, their breath was so bad, I think it made Caesar faint.

CASSIUS: But wait, I ask you. You say Caesar fainted?

CASCA: He fell down and foamed at the mouth and couldn't talk.

BRUTUS: I'm not surprised. He has the falling sickness.[9]

CASSIUS: No, Caesar doesn't have it. But you and I
And honest Casca, we have the falling sickness.

CASCA: I don't know what you mean, but I am sure Caesar fell down. If the ragged people did not cheer him like they cheer actors in the theater, I am not a man.

BRUTUS: What did he say when he came to himself?

CASCA: Well, he told the mob that if he'd done anything wrong, he hoped their majesties would understand it was because of his sickness. Three or four women where I stood cried "Ah, good soul!" and forgave him with all their hearts. But that means nothing. They would have done the same thing if he'd stabbed their mothers.

BRUTUS: And after that he went away sad?

CASCA: Yes.

CASSIUS: Did Cicero say anything?

CASCA: Yes, he spoke Greek.

CASSIUS: What did he say?

---

9. the falling sickness epilepsy

CASCA: If I tell you that, I'll never look you in the face
again. Those who understood him smiled at one
another and shook their heads, but it was Greek to
me. I have more news. Flavius and Marullus have
been removed from office for pulling scarves off
Caesar's statues. Good-bye. There was more
foolishness, if I could remember it.

CASSIUS: Will you have dinner with me tomorrow?

CASCA: Yes, if I'm still alive, and if the food's good.

CASSIUS: Good. I will expect you.

CASCA: Do that. Good-bye to you both.

(CASCA *exits.*)

BRUTUS: What a dull fellow he has grown to be!
He was sharp and lively when we were in school.

CASSIUS: And he still is, when it comes to doing
Any job that calls for brave, quick action.
He lets people think he's rude and stupid.
It makes his words go down more easily.

BRUTUS: This is true. I'll say good-bye for now.
Tomorrow, if you want to speak with me,
Come to my house, or I will come to yours.

CASSIUS: I will do so. Till then, think of the world.

(BRUTUS *exits.*)

Well, Brutus, you are noble. Yet I see
Your honorable nature may be turned
From what it wants to do. So it is right
That noble minds always keep with others
That are noble; for whose nobility is so firm
That he cannot be led aside by falseness?
Caesar resents me, but he loves Brutus.

If I were Brutus now, and he were Cassius,
He would not influence me as I have him.
Tonight I will throw letters through his window.
I will disguise my writing, so the letters seem
To come from several people. Each will speak
Of the respect all Rome holds for his name.
They'll also hint at Caesar's great ambition.
After that, let Caesar secure his power,
For we will shake him, or know a darker hour.

(CASSIUS *exits.*)

Scene 3

A street in Rome. Thunder and lightning. CASCA *and* CICERO *enter.*

CICERO: Good evening, Casca. You brought Caesar home?
    Why are you out of breath? Why do you look like
        that?

CASCA: Aren't you moved, Cicero, when all the earth
    Shakes like an unstable thing? I have seen storms
    Whose scolding winds have broken mighty oaks.
    I've seen the ocean swell and rage and foam,
    Ambitious to be raised to join the clouds.
    But never till tonight, never till now,
    Did I go through a fire-dropping storm.
    Either there is a civil war in heaven,
    Or else the world, insulting to the gods,
    Angers them so that they send destruction.

CICERO: Did you see any other wonders?

CASCA: A common slave (you know him well by sight)
    Held up his left hand, and it flamed and burned
    Like twenty torches, yet he was not harmed.

14

And near the Capitol I saw a lion
Who looked at me and then just went on by.
I saw a hundred ghastly, frightened women
Gathered in a crowd, who swore they saw
Men all on fire walking in the streets.
And yesterday an owl sat at noon,
Hooting and shrieking in the marketplace.
When wonders such as these come all at once,
Men cannot speak of them as natural things.
I do believe they carry signs and warnings.

CICERO: Indeed, we live in times that are not normal.
But men may look on such things as they want,
Far from the meaning of the things themselves.
Will Caesar be at the Capitol tomorrow?

CASCA: He will, for he did ask Mark Antony
To let you know he will be there tomorrow.

CICERO: Good night then, Casca. This troubled sky
Should not be walked in.

CASCA: Good-bye, Cicero.

(CICERO *exits.* CASSIUS *enters.*)

CASSIUS: Who's there?

CASCA: A Roman.

CASSIUS: Casca, by your voice.

CASCA: Your ear is good. What a night this is!

CASSIUS: A very pleasing night to honest men.

CASCA: Who ever knew the skies to threaten so?

CASSIUS: Those who know the earth is full of faults.
I have been walking through the streets awhile,
Exposing my body to the dangerous night.
You see, I've bared my chest before the thunder.

And when the lightning flashed, I gave myself
To the very flash of it.

CASCA: But why? It is men's place to fear and tremble
When mighty gods send us such scary signs,
And not to challenge them.

CASSIUS: You are dull, Casca. You don't have, or use
The spark of life that should be in a Roman.
You look pale, and show such fear and wonder
At the strange signs before us in the sky.
But if you would consider the true cause
Of all these fires, all these gliding ghosts,
Of why things change from their natural states,
You'd find that heaven brought about these things
To warn us of a monster in our midst.
Now, Casca, I could name somebody
Most like this dreadful night.
He thunders, flashes, opens graves, and roars
Just like the lion in the Capitol.
He is no mightier than you or I,
But, like these signs, he has grown strange and
  frightening.

CASCA: It's Caesar you mean, isn't it, Cassius?

CASSIUS: Let it be who it is. For Romans now
Are flesh and blood just like their ancestors.
But, sad to tell, our fathers' minds are dead,
And we are governed by our mothers' spirits.
We serve and obey as if we were women.

CASCA: Indeed, they say the Senators mean
To set up Caesar as a king tomorrow.

CASSIUS: If they do, then Cassius, with this dagger,
Shall free himself from slavery.

(He holds his knife pointed at his own chest.)

> By this, you gods, you make the weak most strong.
> By this, you gods, you free us from our chains.
> No prison walls can hold the strength of spirit.
> But life, tired of the bars of this world,
> Always has the power to end itself.
> If I know this, let all the world know it.
> That part of tyranny[10] that I bear,
> I can shake off as I wish.

CASCA: So can I.
> Every slave holds in his own hand
> The power to free himself from slavery.

CASSIUS: And why should Caesar be a tyrant, then?
> I know he only makes himself a wolf
> Because he knows the Romans to be sheep.
> Those who would quickly build a mighty fire
> Begin it with weak straws. What trash is Rome,
> What garbage, when it lets itself be fuel
> To light up so vile a thing as Caesar?
> But my feelings, where have you led me?
> I may be talking to a willing slave.
> If so, I must answer for what I've said.
> But I am armed, and not bothered by danger.

CASCA: You speak to Casca. I'm no grinning tell-tale.
> Now wait. My hand. *(They shake hands.)*
> Don't give up your cause,
> And I will set this foot of mine as far
> As he who goes the farthest.

CASSIUS: There's a bargain made.

---

10. tyranny   rule by a tyrant, one who uses power cruelly and unjustly

Now, you should know, I have already moved
To bring some of the noblest-minded Romans
Into this honorable but dangerous plan.
They're waiting for me now at Pompey's Porch.[11]
For on this fearful night, no one is walking
In the streets. The weather shows a face
As bloody, fiery, and terrible as our work.

(CINNA *enters.*)

CASCA: Stand close. Someone is coming in a hurry.

CASSIUS: It's Cinna; I can tell him by his walk.
    He is a friend. Cinna, where are you hurrying to?

CINNA: To find you. Who's that? Metellus Cimber?

CASSIUS: No, it is Casca, someone closely tied
    To our plan. Are they waiting for me, Cinna?

CINNA: I am glad of it. What a fearful night!
    Two or three of us have seen strange sights.

CASSIUS: Are they waiting for me? Tell me.

CINNA: Yes, they are. Oh, Cassius, if you could
    Just win the noble Brutus to our side—

CASSIUS: Don't worry. Good Cinna, take this paper.
    Be sure to lay it on the Praetor's chair[12]
    Where Brutus must find it. Then throw this one
    Into his window. Set this third one up
    With wax on the statue of old Brutus.
    When you're done, go back to Pompey's Porch.
    Are Decius Brutus and Trebonius there?

CINNA: All but Metellus Cimber, and he's gone

---

11. **Pompey's Porch**   a platform near a theater built by
    Pompey
12. **Praetor's chair**   judge's chair (Brutus held the office of
    praetor, or judge)

To look for you at your house. Well, I'll hurry
And go and leave these papers where you told me.

CASSIUS: And afterward, return to Pompey's Theater.

(CINNA *exits.*)

Come, Casca. Before morning, you and I
Will go to Brutus's house. Three-fourths of him
Is ours already, and the rest of him
Will be ours at our next meeting.

CASCA: He sits so high in all the people's hearts.
Things that would be crimes if we did them,
Would change with his support, as if by magic,
To something noble and most honorable.

CASSIUS: Him and his worth and our great need of him
You have figured out well. Come, let us go.
It is after midnight, and before morning
We will awake him and be sure of him.

(*They exit.*)

Act 2

Scene 1

The garden of Brutus's home. BRUTUS *enters.*

BRUTUS: Lucius? Hey there, Lucius?
    I cannot see how far the stars have moved;
    I cannot guess how close it is to day.
    —Lucius, where are you?—I wish I had
    The fault of sleeping soundly. Wake up, Lucius!

(LUCIUS *enters.*)

LUCIUS: You called, my lord?

BRUTUS: Light a candle in my study, Lucius.
    When you have lit it, come and call me here.

LUCIUS: I will, my lord.

(*He exits.*)

BRUTUS: It must be by his death. I myself
    Have no reason to strike out at him,
    Except the public good. He wants to be crowned.
    The question is, how would it change his nature?
    I know that it would put a sting in him
    With which he could do danger as he wished.
    Greatness is abused when it removes
    Remorse from power. Now, I know that Caesar
    Never lets his feelings rule his mind.
    But so often it happens that a good, fair man
    Climbing ambition's ladder, gains the top
    And forgets the hard steps that brought him there.
    So Caesar may. But since he hasn't yet,
    The question is, would he be likely to?

And if so, it may be best to think of him
As a snake's egg, and kill him in the shell.

(LUCIUS *enters, holding a letter.*)

LUCIUS: I left the candle burning in your room, sir.
I found this sealed-up letter by the window.

BRUTUS (*taking the letter*): Is not tomorrow, boy, the ides of March?

LUCIUS: Yes, sir, it is.

BRUTUS: Go back to bed again. It's not yet day.

LUCIUS: I will, sir.

(LUCIUS *exits.*)

BRUTUS: These meteors, whizzing in the air,
Give so much light that I may read by them.

(*He opens the letter and reads.*)

Brutus, You're asleep. Awake and see yourself!
Shall Rome, etc.¹ Speak, strike, put right!
I must fill in what has been left unsaid.
Shall Rome stand under one man's rule? My Rome?
My ancestors drove the last king from its streets.
Am I asked here to speak and strike? Oh, Rome!
I promise you, if that will put things right,
You shall receive all that you ask of Brutus.

(LUCIUS *enters.*)

LUCIUS: Sir, someone knocks.

BRUTUS: Go to the gate. (LUCIUS *exits.*)
Since Cassius first spoke against Caesar to me,

---

1. **etc.** pronounced as if written out, "et cetera"

I have not slept. Between the first idea
Of something dreadful, and the doing of it,
All is nightmare. The spirit and the body
Argue together, and the state of man
Is like a kingdom struck by civil war.

(LUCIUS *enters.*)

LUCIUS: Sir, Cassius is at the door,
Wishing to see you. There are others with him.

BRUTUS: Do you know them?

LUCIUS: No, sir. Their hats are pulled down low,
And half their faces buried in their cloaks.

BRUTUS: Let them come in. (LUCIUS *exits.*)
Oh, conspiracy![2] Are you ashamed
To show your dangerous face by dark of night?
How, then, will you by day find a hole so dark
To hide your monstrous form? Don't look for one.
Hide it instead in smiles and friendliness.
For if you would walk on, and show yourself,
Not even the land of death is dark enough
To keep you from being seen.

(*The Conspirators[3] enter:* CASSIUS, CASCA, DECIUS, CINNA,
METELLUS, *and* TREBONIUS.)

CASSIUS: Good morning, Brutus. Do we trouble you?
I fear we have intruded on your rest.

BRUTUS: No, I was up. I've been awake all night.
Do I know these men who have come with you?

CASSIUS: Yes, every one of them. And there's not one

---

2. conspiracy a secret agreement to do something wrong
3. conspirators those who join in a conspiracy

Who does not honor you. And they all wish
You only thought as highly of yourself
As every noble Roman thinks of you.
This is Trebonius.

BRUTUS: He is welcome here.

CASSIUS: This, Decius Brutus.

BRUTUS: He is welcome too.

CASSIUS: This, Casca; this, Cinna; and this, Metellus
  Cimber.

BRUTUS: They're all welcome. What keeps you awake?

CASSIUS: Could I ask you for a word in private?

(BRUTUS and CASSIUS whisper.)

DECIUS: This way is east. Is that the day breaking?

CASCA: No.

CINNA: Pardon, sir, it is, and those gray lines
  That lace the clouds are messengers of day.

CASCA: You will admit that you are both mistaken.
  Here, where I point my sword, the sun will rise
  Today, in this young season of the year.
  Two months from now, it will be rising there,
  Due east, above the Capitol.

BRUTUS (coming forward with CASSIUS): Give me your
  hands, all of you, one by one.

CASSIUS: And let us swear our resolution.

BRUTUS: No, let's not swear. If men's faces,
  The suffering of our souls, the times we live in
  Are not strong reasons, let us end this now.
  Let's all go home; let tyranny run free,
  Till each of us dies by the tyrant's whim.

But if these reasons are themselves enough
To make us brave (and I am sure they are),
Why should we swear? We need no other bond
To spur us to take action. We are Romans
Who have spoken honestly to other Romans
That this shall be, or we will die for it.
Oaths are for cowards, priests, and cautious men
Who suffer wrongs in silence. Let us not stain
The honest, manly rightness of our cause
Or our unbreakable spirits with an oath.

CASSIUS: Now, what of Cicero? Shall we talk to him?
I think he will stand very strong with us.

CASCA: Let's not leave him out.

METELLUS: No, by no means,
For his gray hairs will buy us good opinion.
Men will say his judgment ruled our hands.
No sign of our wild youth will appear.
It will be buried in his age and dignity.

BRUTUS: No, let's not ask him. Hide our plan from him,
For Cicero will never follow anything
That someone else begins.

CASSIUS: Then leave him out.

CASCA: Indeed, he is not fit.

DECIUS: Shall anyone else be touched, or only Caesar?

CASSIUS: Good point, Decius. I don't think it's wise
For Mark Antony, whom Caesar loves so much,
To outlive Caesar. Antony's too clever.
You know his ways. If he puts them to use,
He will make trouble for us. To prevent it,
Let Antony and Caesar fall together.

BRUTUS: No, Caius Cassius. We will seem too bloody.

Why hack the limbs once the head is cut off?
For Antony is just a limb of Caesar.
Let's be sacrificers, Cassius, not butchers.
Our fight is against the spirit of Caesar.
I wish that we could get at Caesar's spirit
And not harm Caesar! I'm sorry that can't be.
Caesar must bleed for it. Noble friends,
Let's kill him boldly, but not in anger.
Let's carve him as a dish fit for the gods,
Not cut him up as meat to feed our dogs.
And let our hearts, the way good masters do,
Stir up their servants to an act of rage,
And scold them gently after. This will make
The common people see that what we do
Is not done out of envy, but is necessary.
Let us be called cleansers, not murderers.
As for Mark Antony, don't bother with him.
For he can do no more harm than Caesar's arm
When Caesar's head is off.

CASSIUS: Yet I do fear him,
Because of the firm love he has for Caesar.

BRUTUS: No, good Cassius, do not think of him.
If he loves Caesar, all that he can do
Is kill himself, to die for Caesar.
And this is more than I expect of him.
He lives too much for fun, for sports and parties.

TREBONIUS: There's no reason to fear him. Let him live,
And he will laugh about this afterward.

(*A clock strikes.*)

CASSIUS: The clock has struck three times.

TREBONIUS: It's time to go.

CASSIUS: Wait. How can we be sure
That Caesar will even leave his house today?
For he has grown quite superstitious lately,
Quite different from the way he used to feel
About ceremonies, fantasies, and dreams.
It may be that the wonders of this night,
Combined with what the augurers[4] might say,
Will keep him from the Capitol today.

DECIUS: Don't worry. If that's what Caesar thinks,
I can change his mind. He loves to hear
That charging unicorns may be fooled by trees,
Bears by mirrors, elephants by traps,
Lions by nets, and men by flatterers.
But when I tell him he hates flatterers,
He says he does, being then most flattered.
Let me do the job. For I can bend his mood
In our direction, and bring him to the Capitol.

CASSIUS: No, we will all be there to bring him.

METELLUS: Caius Ligarius has a grudge against Caesar,
Who raged at him for speaking well of Pompey.
Has anyone thought of asking him to join us?

BRUTUS: Now, good Metellus, you go to his house.
He's a good friend of mine, and owes me favors.
Send him to me, and I will talk to him.

CASSIUS: Morning is near. We'll leave you, Brutus.
Friends, go your ways. But all of you remember
What we have said, and show that you are Romans.

BRUTUS: Good gentlemen, be careful how you look.
Don't let your faces give away our purpose.

---

4. augurers Roman religious officials whose job was to read
the future

Be like actors. Don't seem tired or worried.
And now, good-bye to every one of you.

(*All but* BRUTUS *exit.*)

Boy! Lucius! Fast asleep? It does not matter.
Enjoy the honey-heavy dew of sleep.
You have no worries keeping you awake.

(PORTIA *enters.*)

PORTIA: Brutus, my lord.

BRUTUS: Portia! What's the matter? You're up early.
It's not good for your health to be awake
And outside on this raw, cold morning.

PORTIA: Nor for yours, either, Brutus. You have stolen
Out of my bed. And last night, at supper,
You suddenly got up and walked around
Thinking and sighing, with your arms crossed.
And when I asked you what the matter was,
You stared at me with cruel, angry looks.
I asked you again, and you scratched your head,
And stamped your foot impatiently.
Still I insisted; still you did not answer.
Instead, with an angry wave of your hand,
You told me I should leave. And so I did.
I was afraid to increase your impatience.
It seemed too strong already, and I hoped
That it was just a mood that came upon you.
It will not let you talk, nor eat, nor sleep.
If it changed your face as it has your behavior,
I would not then know you to be Brutus.
Dear husband, tell me what is troubling you.

BRUTUS: I am not feeling well, and that is all.

PORTIA: Brutus is wise. If he were feeling sick,
　　He would be seeking ways to become well.

BRUTUS: And so I am. Portia, go to bed.

PORTIA: Is Brutus sick? And is it good for health
　　To walk around half-dressed in the damp air
　　Of early morning? What, is Brutus sick,
　　And sneaking out of his warm bed at night
　　To breathe the chilly air? No, Brutus.
　　You have some disorder in your mind,
　　And I, by my place as your wife,
　　Should know about it. (*She kneels.*) On my knees,
　　I beg you, by the beauty you once saw in me,
　　By all your words of love, and that great vow
　　Which made us one. Tell me, your self, your half,
　　Why you are heavy. Tell me what men tonight
　　Have come to see you, six or seven of them,
　　Who hid their faces even from the darkness.

BRUTUS: Don't kneel, noble Portia. (*He lifts her up.*)

PORTIA: I would not need to, if you were noble Brutus.
　　Is there exception to the bond of marriage
　　That you should keep your secrets from me now?
　　Am I your self, but only within limits?
　　To eat your meals with you, comfort your bed,
　　And talk to you sometimes? If it be no more,
　　Portia is Brutus's harlot, not his wife.

BRUTUS: You are my true and honorable wife,
　　As dear to me as every drop of blood
　　That runs through my sad heart.

PORTIA: If this were so, then I would know your secret.
　　I am a woman, yes, but even so,
　　A woman that Lord Brutus chose as wife.

I am a woman, yes, but even so,
A woman well-respected, Cato's[5] daughter.
Do you think I am an ordinary woman,
Having such a father and such a husband?
Tell me your secrets; I will not disclose them.
I have made strong proof of my self-control.
I have willingly given myself a wound
Here, in the thigh. Can I bear that with patience
And not my husband's secrets?

BRUTUS: Oh, you gods,
Make me worthy of this noble wife!
(*Knocking from offstage.*)
Listen, someone's here. Portia, go inside,
And very soon your heart will know my secrets.
All my business I'll explain to you,
All that is written on my sad face.
Leave me now, quickly.

(PORTIA *exits.*)

Lucius, who's that knocking?

(LUCIUS *and* LIGARIUS *enter.*)

LUCIUS: Here is a sick man who wants to talk to you.

BRUTUS: Caius Ligarius, whom Metellus spoke of.
Boy, step aside.

(LUCIUS *exits.*)

Caius Ligarius, how are you?

LIGARIUS: Please accept greetings from a weak tongue.

---

5. Cato Marcus Portius Cato, a respected Roman statesman
who took Pompey's side against Caesar and killed himself
when Pompey was defeated

BRUTUS: What a time you've chosen to be sick!

LIGARIUS: I am not sick, if Brutus wants me here
For any task that's worth the name of honor.

BRUTUS: Such a task I have, Ligarius,
If you were only well enough to hear it.

LIGARIUS: By all the gods that Romans bow before,
I here throw off my sickness. Soul of Rome,
Brave son of honorable ancestors,
You have, as if by magic, healed my spirit.
Ask me now to run, and I will fight
Against impossible things. Yes, even win.
What must be done?

BRUTUS: A piece of work that will make sick men
whole.

LIGARIUS: But isn't there one whole we must make
sick?

BRUTUS: We must do that too. What it is, my Caius,
I shall tell you while we're on our way
To whom we do it to.

LIGARIUS: Let's go, then,
With my heart newly fired, I follow you.
I don't know where we're going, but it's enough
That Brutus leads me.

(*Thunder is heard.*)

BRUTUS: Follow me, then.

(*They exit.*)

Scene 2

Caesar's house. Thunder and lightning. CAESAR *enters in his nightgown.*

CAESAR: Neither heaven nor earth have been at peace
    tonight.
    Three times Calpurnia has cried out in her sleep,
    "Help, help, they murder Caesar"—Who is there?

(A SERVANT *enters.)*

SERVANT: My lord.

CAESAR: Go tell the priests to make a sacrifice
    And bring me their opinions of success.

SERVANT: I will, my lord.

(He exits. CALPURNIA *enters.)*

CALPURNIA: What is this, Caesar? Where are you going?
    You shall not stir out of this house today.

CAESAR: Caesar shall go out. They who threaten me
    Look only at my back. When they see
    The face of Caesar, they all disappear.

CALPURNIA: Caesar, I never believed in omens,
    Yet now they scare me. One of our servants
    Reports most horrid sights seen by the guards,
    Besides the things that we have heard and seen.
    A lioness gave birth to cubs in the streets.
    Graves have opened, giving up their dead.
    Fierce, fiery warriors fought up in the clouds
    And rained blood upon the Capitol.
    The noise of battle was heard in the air—
    Horses neighed, and dying men did groan.
    Oh, Caesar, all these things are very strange,

And I do fear them.

CAESAR: What can be avoided
When the mighty gods have formed their purpose?
Yet Caesar shall go out, because these signs
May be for anyone, not just for Caesar.

CALPURNIA: When beggars die, there are no comets seen;
The heavens themselves blaze forth the death of
princes.

CAESAR: Cowards die many times before their deaths;
The valiant[6] never taste of death but once.
Of all the wonders I have ever heard,
The strangest seems to me that men fear death.
Since death is a necessary end,
It will come when it will come.

(*The* SERVANT *enters.*)

What do the augurers say?

SERVANT: They want you not to stir outside today.
Pulling the insides from their sacrifice,
They could not find a heart inside the beast.

CAESAR: The gods do this to shame cowardice.
Caesar would be a beast without a heart
If he should stay at home today for fear.
No, Caesar shall not. Danger knows full well
That Caesar is more dangerous than he.
We are two lions littered in one day,
And I the elder and more terrible.
And Caesar shall go out.

CALPURNIA: Oh, my lord,
Your confidence eats up your wisdom.

---

6. valiant brave

Do not go out today. Call it my fear
That keeps you in the house, and not your own.
We'll send Mark Antony to the Senate House,
And he shall say you are not well today.
Let me, upon my knee, win this from you.

(*She kneels.*)

CAESAR: Mark Antony shall say I am not well,
And for your sake, I will stay at home.

(*He lifts her up.* DECIUS *enters.*)

Here's Decius Brutus. He shall tell them so.

DECIUS: Hail, Caesar. Good morning, worthy Caesar.
I come to bring you to the Senate House.

CAESAR: And you come at the very best of times
To bring my greetings to the Senators.
Tell them that I will not come today.
"Cannot" is false; "I dare not", even falser.
I will not come today. Tell them so, Decius.

CALPURNIA: Say he is sick.

CAESAR: Shall Caesar send a lie?
Have I reached out my arm so far in conquest
To be afraid to tell old men the truth?
Decius, go tell them Caesar will not come.

DECIUS: Most mighty Caesar, let me know some cause,
So they won't laugh at me when I tell them.

CAESAR: The cause is in my will. I will not come.
That is enough to satisfy the Senate.
But privately, because you are my friend,
I'll tell you. Calpurnia keeps me home.
She dreamed last night she saw my statue,
Which, like a fountain with a hundred spouts,

Did run pure blood. And many joyful Romans
Came smiling to bathe their hands in it.
She sees this as a warning from the gods
That evil is upon me. On her knee
She begged me to stay home with her today.

DECIUS: But you've interpreted[7] this dream all wrong!
It is a dream both good and fortunate.
Your statue spouting blood from many pipes,
In which so many smiling Romans bathed,
Means that your blood will revive Rome,
And many great men will come to you for favors.
This is the meaning of Calpurnia's dream.

CAESAR: And this way, too, you have explained it well.

DECIUS: I have, when you hear what I have to say.
Now know this: The Senate has decided
To give a crown to mighty Caesar today.
They may change their minds if you don't come.
Besides, how would it be if someone said,
"Break up the Senate till another time,
When Caesar's wife shall have a better dream"?
If Caesar hides himself, will they not whisper,
"Caesar is afraid"? Pardon me, Caesar,
My love for you makes me tell you this,
And makes me lose my sense of what is right.

CAESAR: How foolish do your fears seem now, Calpurnia!
I am ashamed that I gave in to them.
Give me my robe, for I will go.

(BRUTUS, LIGARIUS, METELLUS, CASCA, TREBONIUS, CINNA,
and PUBLIUS enter.)

And here is Publius to bring me there.

---

7. interpreted explained the meaning of

PUBLIUS: Good morning, Caesar.

CAESAR: Welcome, Publius.
What, Brutus, are you up so early too?
Good morning, Casca. Caius Ligarius,
I was never so much your enemy
As that sickness which made you so thin.
What time is it?

BRUTUS: Caesar, it has struck eight.

CAESAR: I thank you for your trouble and courtesy.

(ANTONY *enters*.)

See, even Antony, who celebrates all night long,
Is up and ready. Good morning, Antony.

ANTONY: And to you, most noble Caesar.

CAESAR (*to the* SERVANT): Have them get ready.
It will be my fault if we are late.

(SERVANT *exits*.)

Now, Cinna—Now, Metellus and Trebonius,
I have an hour's talk in store for you.
Remember that you call on me today.
Be near me that I may remember you.

TREBONIUS: Caesar, I will. (*Aside*[8]) I will be so near
That your friends shall wish I had been further.

CAESAR: My friends, go in and taste some wine with me,
And then, like friends, we all shall go together.

BRUTUS (*aside*): Not all that seems alike is really the same.

---

8. **aside** a term used in plays to indicate that the speaker's
words are meant just for the audience and cannot be heard by
any of the other characters

Oh, Caesar, my heart is sad to think of it.

(*They exit.*)

Scene 3

A street. ARTEMIDORUS *enters, reading a letter.*

ARTEMIDORUS: *Caesar, beware of Brutus. Be warned of
Cassius. Don't come near Casca. Watch out for Cinna.
Don't trust Trebonius. Notice Metellus Cimber. Decius
Brutus does not like you. You have wronged Caius
Ligarius. There is one mind in all these men, and it is
turned against Caesar. Look around. Thinking that
you're safe opens the way to conspiracy. May the gods
defend you!*

> Your friend,
> Artemidorus

I will stand here till Caesar comes along,
And as a citizen I will give him this.
My heart is sad that honor cannot live
Out of reach of envy.
If you read this, good Caesar, you may live.
If not, the fates⁹ are on the side of traitors.

(ARTEMIDORUS *exits.*)

Scene 4

PORTIA *and* LUCIUS *enter.*

PORTIA: Boy, run to the Senate House.
Don't ask me why, just go. Why do you stay?
LUCIUS: To know my errand, madam.

---

9. **the fates**   three goddesses whom Romans believed decided
the course of life

PORTIA: I would have had you there and back again
Before I could tell you what you should do there.
(*Aside*) Oh, self-control, stay with me.
Set a huge mountain between my heart and tongue!
How hard it is for women to keep secrets!
(*To* LUCIUS) Are you still here?

LUCIUS: Madam, what should I do?
Run to the Capitol, and nothing else?
And then return to you, and nothing else?

PORTIA: Bring me word, boy, if your lord looks well.
And see what Caesar does, and who stands near him.
Listen, boy, what noise is that?

LUCIUS: I don't hear any noise.

PORTIA: Then listen well. I think I hear a fight.
The wind brings the sound from the Capitol.

LUCIUS: Truly, madam, I hear nothing.

(*The* SOOTHSAYER *enters.*)

PORTIA: Come here, fellow. Where are you coming from?

SOOTHSAYER: From my own house, good lady.

PORTIA: Has Caesar yet gone to the Capitol?

SOOTHSAYER: Not yet, Madam. I'm going to wait for him
To see him pass on to the Capitol.

PORTIA: You have some suit[10] for Caesar, is that right?

SOOTHSAYER: Yes I have, lady. If Caesar will hear me,
I shall plead with him to befriend himself.

PORTIA: Why, do you know of any harm meant toward him?

SOOTHSAYER: None that I know; much that I fear.

---

10. suit formal request to a government official

Good morning to you. Here the street is narrow.
The crowd that follows Caesar at his heels
Will crowd a weak old man almost to death.
I'll find a place less crowded. There I'll wait,
And speak to Caesar as he comes along.

(*The* SOOTHSAYER *exits.*)

PORTIA: I must go in. (*Aside*) Oh, Brutus,
  May the gods help you in your plan!
  Oh, the boy heard me. (*To* LUCIUS) Brutus has a suit
  That Caesar will not grant. Run, Lucius.
  Tell my lord that I am in good spirits,
  And bring me word of what he says to you.

(*They exit separately.*)

Act 3

Scene 1

A street near the Senate House. Trumpets sound. CAESAR, ANTONY, LEPIDUS; BRUTUS, CASSIUS, CASCA, DECIUS, METELLUS, TREBONIUS, CINNA; PUBLIUS, POPILIUS, ARTEMIDORUS, *the* SOOTHSAYER, *and other* SENATORS *and* SUITORS *enter.*

CAESAR (*to the* SOOTHSAYER): The ides of March are come.

SOOTHSAYER: Yes, Caesar, but not gone.

ARTEMIDORUS: Hail, Caesar. Read this document.

DECIUS: Trebonius wishes you to read his suit
    At your convenience.

ARTEMIDORUS: Oh, Caesar, read mine first, for my suit
    Concerns you more directly. Read it, great Caesar.

CAESAR: What concerns myself shall be read last.

ARTEMIDORUS: Don't delay, Caesar; read it at once.

CAESAR: What, is this fellow mad?

PUBLIUS: Sir, step aside.

CASSIUS: Why do you urge your suit here in the street?
    Come to the Capitol.

(CAESAR *goes forward, the rest following.*)

POPILIUS (*to* CASSIUS): I wish luck to your plan today.

CASSIUS: What plan, Popilius?

POPILIUS: Good-bye.

BRUTUS: What did he say?

CASSIUS: He wished us luck. I fear we are found out.

BRUTUS: Look, he's going to Caesar. Watch him.

CASSIUS: Casca, be quick, or we may be stopped.
Brutus, what shall we do? If Caesar knows,
Either he or Cassius will never go home,
For I will kill myself.

BRUTUS: Cassius, be calm.
Popilius is not telling Caesar of our plan.
Look, he's smiling, and Caesar does not change.

(TREBONIUS *and* ANTONY *exit.*)

CASSIUS: Trebonius knows it's time. Look, Brutus.
He draws Mark Antony out of the way.

DECIUS: Where is Metellus Cimber? Now's the time
For him to go present his suit to Caesar.

CINNA: Casca, you are the first to raise your hand.

(*They enter the Senate House.*)

CAESAR: Are we all ready? Tell me now the problems
That Caesar and his Senate must put right.

METELLUS (*kneeling*): Most high and mighty Caesar,
Metellus Cimber throws his heart before you.

CAESAR: I must stop you, Cimber. These low bows
Might move ordinary men to change the laws
That they have made. And our laws would become
Nothing more than rules in children's games.
Do not be foolish. I will not be changed
By sweet words, bows, and dog-like fawning.
It was my will your brother should be banished.
If you now bow and pray and beg for him,
I'll kick you out of my way like a dog.
Know that Caesar does not act unjustly,
And will not change his mind without just cause.

METELLUS: Is there no voice more worthy than my own
    To speak to Caesar for my banished brother?

BRUTUS (*kneeling*): I kiss your hand, but not in flattery,
    Caesar.
    I ask that Publius Cimber be brought home.

CAESAR: What, Brutus?

CASSIUS (*kneeling*): Pardon, Caesar. Caesar, pardon!
    As low as to your foot does Cassius fall
    To beg for Publius Cimber's freedom.

CAESAR: I could be moved by this, were I like you.
    If I could beg others, begging would move me.
    But I am as constant as the Northern Star.
    The skies are painted with a million sparks.
    They are all fire, and every one does shine,
    But there is only one that holds its place.
    The world is like that: furnished well with men,
    All are flesh and blood, and all have thought.
    Yet of them all, I know of only one
    Whose will cannot be shaken. I am he.
    Let me show it, even in this matter.
    I was firm that Cimber should be banished,
    And I do remain firm to keep him so.

CINNA (*kneeling*): Oh, Caesar—

CAESAR: Away! Do you think you can lift up a mountain?

DECIUS (*kneeling*): Great Caesar—

CAESAR: Does not even Brutus kneel uselessly?

CASCA: Speak, hands, for me!

(CASCA *stabs* CAESAR. *The others rise up and stab*
CAESAR. BRUTUS *is last.*)

CAESAR: Et tu, Brutè?[1] Then fall, Caesar.

(*He dies.*)

CINNA: Liberty! Freedom! Tyranny is dead!
Run, announce it! Cry it in the streets!

CASSIUS: Some of you go to the speaking platforms
And cry out "Liberty and freedom!"

BRUTUS: People and senators, do not be afraid.
Don't run; stay calm. Ambition has been punished.

CASCA: Go to the platform, Brutus.

DECIUS: And Cassius too.

BRUTUS: Where's Publius?

CINNA: Here, and quite confused by all this uproar.

METELLUS: Be ready to fight together, all of us,
In case some friend of Caesar's—

BRUTUS: Don't talk of fighting. Publius, good cheer.
We mean no harm to you, or other Romans.

CASSIUS: Go tell them, Publius. And take good care
That the people, rushing at us, don't hurt you.

BRUTUS: Let no man pay for this but us, the doers.

(*All but the Conspirators exit.* TREBONIUS *enters.*)

CASSIUS: Where is Antony?

TREBONIUS: Fled to his house, stunned.
Men, women, children stare, cry out, and run
As if the world were coming to an end.

BRUTUS: Fates, we will soon know what you wish.
We know that we shall die. It's just the time,

---

1. **Et tu, Brutè?** And you, Brutus?

The drawing out of days, that men care about.

CASCA: Why, he that cuts off twenty years of life
Cuts off so many years of fearing death.

BRUTUS: That being so, then we are Caesar's friends.
We have cut short his time of fearing death.
Stoop, Romans, stoop, and let us bathe
Our hands in Caesar's blood up to the elbows,
And smear our swords. Then we shall walk forth,
And, waving our red weapons over our heads,
Let's all cry "Peace, freedom, and liberty!"

CASSIUS: Stoop, then, and wash.

(*They smear their hands and swords with Caesar's blood.*)

How many ages in the future,
In countries and in languages not yet born,
Will our great scene be acted on the stage?
So often as it is, the group of us
Will be called men who gave their country freedom.

DECIUS: What now? Shall we go?

CASSIUS: Yes, every man.
Brutus shall lead the way, and we will follow,
The boldest and best hearts of Rome.

(*Antony's* SERVANT *enters.*)

BRUTUS: Wait, who comes here? A friend of Antony's?

SERVANT (*kneeling*): Like this, Brutus, my master said to
kneel.
Like this Mark Antony said I should fall down.
And kneeling here, say this:
Brutus is noble, wise, brave, and honest.
Caesar was mighty, brave, royal, and loving.

Say, I love Brutus, and I honor him.
Say, I feared Caesar, honored him, and loved him.
If Brutus will let Antony come here in safety,
And tell him why Caesar deserved death,
Then Antony promises Brutus due respect.
He shall love Brutus living more than Caesar dead,
And will help guide Brutus through the dangers
That he will face along this path he's chosen.

BRUTUS: Your master is a wise and valiant Roman.
I never thought him worse.
Tell him to come here, if it pleases him.
He shall have what he asks, and by my honor,
He shall not be harmed.

SERVANT: I'll get him now.

(*Antony's* SERVANT *exits.*)

BRUTUS: I know that we will have him as our friend.

CASSIUS: I hope we may, and yet I fear him still.

(ANTONY *enters.*)

BRUTUS: But here comes Antony. Welcome, Mark Antony.

ANTONY: Oh, mighty Caesar, do you lie so low?
Are all your conquests, glories, honors, riches
Shrunk down to this small size? Good-bye, then.
I don't know, gentlemen, what you intend.
Who else must die? Who else has grown too big?
If I am one, there is no better time
Than Caesar's death hour, and no weapons
Half as fit as these, your swords, made rich
With the most noble blood of all this world.
I ask you, if you think I am your enemy,
Do as you please now, while your bloody hands

Still reek and smoke. If I live a thousand years,
I'll never find a better place to die
Than here by Caesar, nor a better way
Than killed by you, the spirits of our age.

BRUTUS: Antony, don't beg your death from us!
I know we must appear bloody and cruel.
You see our hands, and see what they have done.
But you can't see our hearts, and they are full
Of pity. As fire drives out fire,
So one pity drives away another.
Our pity for the wrongs that Rome has suffered
Has done this deed to Caesar. But for you,
Mark Antony, our swords have blunted points.
Our arms, though bloody, welcome you as a friend;
Our hearts, with all kind love, in brotherhood.

CASSIUS: Your voice shall be as strong as any man's
In choosing who shall run the government.

BRUTUS: Just be patient, till we have quieted
The people, now beside themselves with fear.
And then we will be glad to give the reason
Why I killed Caesar, even though I loved him.

ANTONY: I don't doubt your wisdom.
Let every man give me his bloody hand.
First, Marcus Brutus, I will shake with you.
Next, Caius Cassius, I take your hand.
Now, Decius Brutus, yours; now yours, Metellus;
Yours, Cinna; and my brave Casca, yours.
Last, though not least in love, yours, Trebonius.
Gentlemen—what can I say that you'll believe?
There are only two ways you can look at me—
Either as a coward or a flatterer.
That I did love you, Caesar, oh, it's true!

If your spirit is looking at us now,
It must be harder for you than your death
To see me making peace with those who killed you,
Shaking the bloody fingers of your enemies—
All most noble!—here beside your body.
Had I as many eyes as you have wounds,
Weeping as fast as they stream out your blood,
I would look better than I do in joining
In friendship with these men. Pardon me, Julius!
Here you did fall, and here your hunters stand.
How like a deer struck by many princes
Do you here lie!

CASSIUS: Mark Antony—

ANTONY: Pardon me, Caius Cassius.
The enemies of Caesar will say this.
Why isn't it proper for a friend?

CASSIUS: I do not blame you for praising Caesar,
But what agreement will you make with us?
Shall you be counted as our friend, or not?

ANTONY: That's why I shook your hands. I was only
Swayed a moment when I looked down at Caesar.
I'll be your friend, if you shall give me reasons
Why and how Caesar was dangerous.

BRUTUS: Or else we would seem to be savages.
Our reasons, Antony, are so worthy,
That if you were the son of Caesar,
You would be satisfied.

ANTONY: That's all I want.
And I ask you also if I may
Bring his body to the marketplace
And, as a friend, speak at his funeral.

BRUTUS: You shall, Mark Antony.

48

CASSIUS: Brutus, a word with you.
(*Aside to* BRUTUS) You don't know what you're doing.
Don't let him speak. Don't you know how the people
Might be stirred up by what he says to them?

BRUTUS (*aside to* CASSIUS): But I'll speak first,
And tell them the reason Caesar died.
They'll know that Antony speaks by our permission,
And that it is our wish that Caesar shall
Have all the rites[2] and honors the dead deserve.
It shall help us more than do us harm.

CASSIUS (*aside to* BRUTUS): I don't know what may
happen. I don't like it.

BRUTUS: Mark Antony, take Caesar's body.
You shall not in your funeral speech blame us,
But you may say all the good you can of Caesar.
Tell them that you speak by our permission.
You will speak from the same platform as I,
After my speech is ended.

ANTONY: That's all I ask.

BRUTUS: Prepare the body, then, and follow us.

(*All but* ANTONY *exit.*)

ANTONY: Oh, pardon me, you bleeding piece of earth,
That I am meek and gentle with these butchers.
You are the ruins of the noblest man
That ever lived in the tide of times.
Woe to the hand that shed this costly blood!
A curse shall fall upon the limbs of men.
Violent civil war shall shake this land.
Blood and cruelty will become so usual

---

2. rites religious ceremonies

That mothers shall smile to see their children
Cut into pieces by the hands of war.
And Caesar's spirit, raging for revenge,
With Ate[3] by his side, shall, like a king,
Cry "Havoc!" and let slip[4] the dogs of war.
Then this foul deed will smell above the earth
With the living dead groaning to be buried.

(*Octavius's* SERVANT *enters.*)

You serve Octavius Caesar, do you not?

SERVANT: I do, Mark Antony.
Caesar wrote for him to come to Rome.
He did receive his letter, and is coming.
He ordered me to tell you—Oh, Caesar!

ANTONY: Your heart is full of grief. Go away and cry.
Emotion, I see, is catching. My eyes too
Begin to water. Is your master coming?

SERVANT: He camps tonight just twenty miles from
Rome.

ANTONY: Ride quickly back and tell him what has
happened.
Here is a mourning Rome, a dangerous Rome.
It is not a safe place for Octavius yet.
Go back and tell him so—but stay awhile.
Help me take the body to the marketplace.
My speech will show me what the people think
About the bloody men who did this deed.
Whatever happens then, you tell Octavius.
Give me a hand.

---

3. **Ate** (AH-tay) the goddess of revenge
4. **havoc** war cry meaning "kill everyone"; **let slip** let loose

(*They exit, carrying Caesar's body.*)

Scene 2

(*The marketplace.* BRUTUS *and* CASSIUS *enter with a crowd of* PLEBEIANS.[5])

PLEBEIANS: We will be satisfied! Let us be satisfied!

BRUTUS: Then follow me and listen to me, friends.
Cassius, you go to the other street
And divide the crowd.
Those that will hear me speak, let them stay here.
Those that follow Cassius, go with him.
And we shall give the people our reasons
For Caesar's death.

FIRST PLEBEIAN: I will hear Brutus speak.

SECOND PLEBEIAN: I will hear Cassius.
We'll then compare their reasons.

(CASSIUS *exits with some of the* PLEBEIANS. BRUTUS *goes up to the speaking platform.*)

THIRD PLEBEIAN: The noble Brutus speaks. Silence.

BRUTUS: Be patient till the end. Romans, countrymen, and friends, hear my words, and be silent that you may hear. Believe me because of my honor, and respect my honor so that you may believe. Judge me by your wisdom, and awaken your senses so that you may be a better judge. If anyone in this crowd was a friend of Caesar's, I say to him that Brutus's love for Caesar was no less than his. If he wants to know why Brutus rose against Caesar, this is my answer: not because I loved Caesar less, but because I loved

---

5. plebeians common people of Rome

Rome more. Would you rather that Caesar were living, and we all died slaves? Or would you have Caesar dead, and live as free men? As Caesar loved me, I weep for him. As he was lucky, I am happy for him. As he was brave, I honor him. But as he was ambitious,[6] I killed him. Who here is so low that he would be a slave? If any, speak, for I have offended him. Who here is so rude that he would not be a Roman? If any, speak, for I have offended him. Who here is so vile that he will not love his country? If any, speak, for I have offended him. I pause for a reply.

PLEBEIANS: None, Brutus, none!

BRUTUS: Then I have offended no one. I have done no more to Caesar than you shall do to Brutus. The deeds of Caesar are written on a scroll in the Capitol. The glory he deserves is not made less, nor are the reasons why he was killed made more.

(ANTONY *and others enter, carrying Caesar's body.*)

Here comes his body, mourned by Mark Antony. Though he had no hand in his death, Antony will gain something from it—a place in the ruling of the republic—as which of you will not? With this I end: As I killed my best friend for the good of Rome, I have the same dagger for myself when it shall please my country to need my death.

PLEBEIANS: Live, Brutus, live, live!

FIRST PLEBEIAN: Bring him home with honor to his house.

SECOND PLEBEIAN: Give him a statue with his ancestors.

---

6. ambitious greedy for power

THIRD PLEBEIAN: Let him be Caesar.

FOURTH PLEBEIAN: Caesar's better parts
Shall be crowned in Brutus.

BRUTUS: My countrymen—

SECOND PLEBEIAN: Silence! Brutus speaks.

FIRST PLEBEIAN: Quiet!

BRUTUS: Good countrymen, let me leave here alone.
For my sake, stay here with Mark Antony.
Honor Caesar's body, and honor the speech
Which, by our permission, Antony will make.
I urge you, please, stay here and listen to him.

(BRUTUS *comes down from the platform and exits.*)

FIRST PLEBEIAN: Stay; let us hear Mark Antony.

THIRD PLEBEIAN: Let him go up to the platform.

PLEBEIANS: We'll hear him. Noble Antony, go up.

ANTONY: For Brutus's sake, I owe you this favor.

(*He goes up to the platform.*)

FOURTH PLEBEIAN: What did he say about Brutus?

THIRD PLEBEIAN: He said for Brutus's sake
He owes us all a favor.

FOURTH PLEBEIAN: He'd better not speak any harm of
Brutus.

FIRST PLEBEIAN: This Caesar was a tyrant.

THIRD PLEBEIAN: Yes, that's certain.
We are blessed that Rome is rid of him.

ANTONY: You honorable Romans—

SECOND PLEBEIAN: Let's hear what Antony has to say.

PLEBEIANS: Quiet! Let us hear him!

ANTONY: Friends, Romans, countrymen, lend me your ears.
I come to bury Caesar, not to praise him.
The evil that men do lives after them;
The good is often buried with their bones.
So let it be with Caesar. The noble Brutus
Has told you Caesar was ambitious.
If this were so, it was a terrible fault,
And terribly has Caesar answered for it.
Here, by permission of Brutus and the rest
(For Brutus is an honorable man;
So are they all, all honorable men),
I come to speak at Caesar's funeral.
He was my friend, noble and fair to me,
But Brutus says he was ambitious,
And Brutus is an honorable man.
He has brought many captives home to Rome,
Whose ransoms filled the public treasury.
Did this in Caesar seem ambitious?
When the poor cried, Caesar wept;
Ambition should be made of sterner stuff.
Yet Brutus says he was ambitious,
And Brutus is an honorable man.
You all saw, at the feast of Lupercal,
Three times I offered him a kingly crown,
Which he three times refused. Was this ambition?
Yet Brutus says he was ambitious,
And Brutus is an honorable man.
I speak not to disprove what Brutus said,
But I am here to speak what I do know.
You all did love him once, not without cause.
What cause now keeps you, then, from mourning him?
Oh judgment, you have fled to mindless beasts,

And men have lost their reason!—Bear with me;
My heart is in the coffin there with Caesar,
And I must pause till it comes back to me.

(*He cries.*)

FIRST PLEBEIAN: I think he makes much sense.

FOURTH PLEBEIAN: You heard his words?
He would not take the crown. It's certain then
That he was not ambitious.

SECOND PLEBEIAN: Caesar has been wronged.

FIRST PLEBEIAN: If so, someone will pay for it.

SECOND PLEBEIAN: Poor Antony; his eyes are red with
crying.

THIRD PLEBEIAN: There's not a nobler man in Rome than
Antony.

FOURTH PLEBEIAN: Now listen. He begins again to speak.

ANTONY: Only yesterday the word of Caesar might
Have stood against the world. Now here he lies.
Oh, masters, if I chose to stir your rage,
I would do Brutus wrong and Cassius wrong.
Better to wrong the dead, myself, and you,
Than to wrong such honorable men.
But I found this in Caesar's private room:
A parchment[7] with his seal. It's Caesar's will,
Which, pardon me, I don't intend to read.
But if the common people were to hear it,
They would go and kiss dead Caesar's wounds
And dip their handkerchiefs in his blood—
Yes, beg a hair of his for memory.

---

7. **parchment**   paper-like material made from sheepskin

56

FOURTH PLEBEIAN: Let's hear the will. Read it, Antony.

PLEBEIANS: The will, the will! Read us Caesar's will!

ANTONY: Patience, noble friends. I must not read it.
It's not right that you know how Caesar loved you.
You are not wood, you are not stones, but men.
To hear the will of Caesar would inflame you.
It's good that you don't know you are his heirs,
For if you did, then what would come from it?

FOURTH PLEBEIAN: Read the will. We'll hear it, Antony.

PLEBEIANS: Yes, read us the will, Caesar's will.

ANTONY: Will you be patient? Will you stay awhile?
I've gone too far in telling you of it.
I fear I wrong the honorable men
Whose daggers have stabbed Caesar.

FOURTH PLEBEIAN: They were traitors. Honorable men!

SECOND PLEBEIAN: They were murderers. The will! Read
the will!

ANTONY: You will force me, then, to read the will?
Then make a ring around great Caesar's body,
And let me show you him who made the will.
Shall I come down? Have I your permission?

PLEBEIANS: Come down! You have permission!

(ANTONY *comes down from the platform.*)

FOURTH PLEBEIAN: A ring; stand around.

FIRST PLEBEIAN: Stand back from the body.

THIRD PLEBEIAN: Make room for the most noble Antony.

PLEBEIANS: Stand back! Room! Move back!

ANTONY: If you have tears, prepare to shed them now.
You all do know this cloak. I remember

The first time Caesar ever put it on.
It was a summer evening in his tent,
The day he overcame the Nervii.[8]
Look, in this place ran Cassius's dagger.
See what a tear the spiteful Casca made.
Through this hole his best friend Brutus stabbed.
And, as he pulled his cursed steel away,
See how the blood of Caesar followed it,
As if it rushed outside to see for sure
If Brutus so unkindly knocked or not.
Judge, Oh, you gods, how dearly Caesar loved him!
This was the most unkindest cut of all.
For when the noble Caesar saw him stab,
Ingratitude,[9] stronger than traitors' arms
Did conquer him. Then burst his mighty heart.
Oh, what a fall there was, my countrymen!
Then you and I and all of us fell down,
While bloody treason rose up over us.
Oh, now you cry, and I know that you feel
The force of pity. These are gracious drops.
Kind souls, you're crying at the sight
Of Caesar's clothing wounded? Now look here.

(ANTONY *lifts Caesar's mantle.*)

Here is the man, ruined, as you see, by traitors.

FIRST PLEBEIAN: Oh, pitiful sight!

SECOND PLEBEIAN: Oh, noble Caesar!

THIRD PLEBEIAN: Oh, terrible day!

FOURTH PLEBEIAN: Oh, most bloody sight!

---

8. Nervii (NER-vee-ee) a tribe conquered by Caesar in 57 B.C.
9. ingratitude lack of thankfulness

SECOND PLEBEIAN: We will be revenged.

PLEBEIANS: Revenge! Let's go! Find them! Burn!
Kill! Let not one traitor live!

ANTONY: Stay, countrymen.

FIRST PLEBEIAN: Quiet, there! Hear the noble Antony.

SECOND PLEBEIAN: We'll hear him, we'll follow him, and
we'll die with him.

ANTONY: Good friends, don't let me stir you up.
They who have done this deed are honorable,
And no doubt have good reasons for their deed.
I'm not here, friends, to steal away your hearts.
I am no fine speaker, as Brutus is.
As you all know, I am a plain, blunt man
Who loved my friend. I only speak plainly.
I tell you that which you yourselves do know.
I must ask these wounds, poor, poor dumb mouths,
To speak for me. But if I were Brutus,
And Brutus were Antony, then there would be an
Antony
Who'd stir your anger. He would put a tongue
In every wound of Caesar that would move
The very stones of Rome to rise in rage.

PLEBEIANS: We'll rise!

FIRST PLEBEIAN: We'll burn Brutus's house!

THIRD PLEBEIAN: Let's go! Seek out the conspirators!

ANTONY: Please hear me, countrymen; let me speak.
Have you forgot the will I told you of?

PLEBEIANS: The will! Let's stay and hear the will!

ANTONY: Here is the will, and under Caesar's seal.
To every Roman citizen he gives,

To each and every man, seventy-five drachmas.[10]

SECOND PLEBEIAN: Noble Caesar! We'll revenge his death!

ANTONY: He's also left you all his tree-lined walks,
And private gardens by the river Tiber.
He leaves them all to you as public parks
For you and all your children to enjoy.
Here was a Caesar! When comes such another?

FIRST PLEBEIAN: Never, never! Come, away, away!
We'll burn his body in the holy place
And use the burning sticks to set fire
To the houses of all the traitors!

THIRD PLEBEIAN: Tear down their houses, benches,
windows, anything!

(*The* PLEBEIANS *exit, carrying Caesar's body.*)

ANTONY: Now let it work. Trouble, you're let loose.
Go which way you will.

(*Octavius's* SERVANT *enters.*)

What is it, fellow?

SERVANT: Sir, Octavius has already come to Rome.
He and Lepidus are at Caesar's house.

ANTONY: I'll go straight there. What perfect timing!
Luck, in this mood, will give us anything.

SERVANT: I heard him say Brutus and Cassius
Have run like madmen through the gates of Rome.

ANTONY: They probably had some warning of the people,
How I had moved them. Bring me to Octavius.

(*They exit.*)

---

10. **drachma** (DRAHK-muh) a silver coin

Scene 3

A street. Enter CINNA *the poet and, after him, the* PLEBEIANS.

CINNA: I dreamed tonight that I did feast with Caesar.
What evil can this mean?
I do not wish to be outside tonight,
But something leads me.

FIRST PLEBEIAN: What is your name?

SECOND PLEBEIAN: Where are you going?

THIRD PLEBEIAN: Where do you live?

FOURTH PLEBEIAN: Are you a married man or a bachelor?

SECOND PLEBEIAN: Answer every man directly.

FIRST PLEBEIAN: Yes, and briefly.

SECOND PLEBEIAN: Yes, and wisely.

THIRD PLEBEIAN: Yes, and truly would be best.

CINNA: What is my name? Where am I going? Where do I live? Am I a married man or a bachelor? Then to answer every man directly and briefly, wisely and truly: wisely, I say I am a bachelor.

SECOND PLEBEIAN: So you're saying that those who marry are fools? You'll get a punch in the mouth from me for that. Go on directly.

CINNA: Directly, I am going to Caesar's funeral.

FIRST PLEBEIAN: As a friend or as an enemy?

CINNA: As a friend.

SECOND PLEBEIAN: That question is answered directly.

FOURTH PLEBEIAN: Where do you live—briefly.

CINNA: Briefly, I live by the Capitol.

THIRD PLEBEIAN: Your name, sir, truly.

CINNA: Truly, my name is Cinna.

FIRST PLEBEIAN: Tear him to pieces! He's a conspirator!

CINNA: I am Cinna the poet, I am Cinna the poet!

FOURTH PLEBEIAN: Tear him for his bad verses! Tear him for his bad verses!

CINNA: I am not Cinna the conspirator!

FOURTH PLEBEIAN: It doesn't matter. His name's Cinna. Pluck the name out of his heart and kill him.

THIRD PLEBEIAN: Tear him, tear him! Come, to Brutus's, to Cassius's; burn all! Some to Decius's house, some to Casca's, some to Metellus Cimber's! Come on, let's go!

(*All the* PLEBEIANS *exit, carrying off* CINNA.)

Act 4

Scene 1

Antony's house. ANTONY, OCTAVIUS, *and* LEPIDUS *enter.*

ANTONY: All these men, then, shall die. Their names are
    marked.

OCTAVIUS: Your brother too must die. Agreed, Lepidus?

LEPIDUS: I do agree.

OCTAVIUS: Mark him down, Antony.

LEPIDUS:—If you agree, Mark Antony, that Publius,
    Your sister's son, also shall not live.

ANTONY: He shall die; with this mark I condemn him.
    But, Lepidus, you go to Caesar's house.
    Bring the will here, and we shall figure out
    How to reduce the amount he left the people.

LEPIDUS: Shall I find you here?

OCTAVIUS: Here, or at the Capitol.

(LEPIDUS *exits.*)

ANTONY: There goes a man of little value,
    Fit to be sent on errands. Is it right
    That he share power equally with us?

OCTAVIUS: So you thought. And so you gave him voice
    In choosing who will live and who will die.

ANTONY: Octavius, I am much older than you.
    We're only laying honors on this man
    To ease ourselves of some share of the blame.
    He'll carry them as a donkey carries gold.
    He'll groan and sweat under the heavy load,

Either led or driven, as we point the way.
And when he's brought our treasure where we want,
Then we'll take down his load and turn him out
To shake his ears and eat grass in the pasture.

OCTAVIUS: You may do what you want,
But he's a brave and proven soldier.

ANTONY: So is my horse, Octavius, and for that
I give him hay. He's something that I teach
To fight, to turn, to stop, to go ahead.
My will controls the movements of his body.
In some ways Lepidus is just like that.
He must be taught and trained and made to go.
He has no imagination. All his tastes
Are out-of-date fashions that other men
Have used and cheapened. Do not think of him
Except as property. And now, Octavius,
To important matters. Brutus and Cassius
Are raising armies. We must act at once.
We must combine our forces, gather our friends.
We must meet to discuss how secret matters
May best be made public, and these dangers faced.

OCTAVIUS: Then let us do so, for our enemies
Are barking all around us. And some friends,
I fear, have mischief in their hearts.

(*They exit.*)

Scene 2

An army camp in Greece. A drum sounds. BRUTUS,
LUCILIUS, LUCIUS, *and* SOLDIERS *enter.* TITINIUS *and*
PINDARUS *meet them.*

64

BRUTUS: Stand!¹ Lucilius, is Cassius nearby?

LUCILIUS: He is here, and his slave Pindarus
Has come to bring you greetings from his master.

BRUTUS: I accept his greeting. Pindarus, your master
Has lately made me wish that things we've done
Could be undone. But if he'll meet with me,
I shall be satisfied.

PINDARUS: I'm sure my noble master will appear.
He regards you well and honors you.

BRUTUS: I do not doubt him. A word, Lucilius.

(BRUTUS *and* LUCILIUS *walk aside.*)

How did he receive you? I must know.

LUCILIUS: Politely and with all due respect,
But not with the friendliness he used to have.

BRUTUS: You describe a friendship that has cooled.
When love begins to sicken and decay,
It uses forced ceremony. There are no tricks
In plain and simple faith. But hollow men
Are like horses hot before a race.

(*Sound of marching feet offstage.*)

They make a brave show and promise spirit,
But when the race begins, their necks bow down,
And, false and broken down, they fail the test.
Is his army coming?

LUCILIUS: They mean to camp tonight in Sardis.²
The greater part have come with Cassius.

---

1. **stand** halt; stop
2. **Sardis** an ancient city near present-day Ismir, Turkey

(CASSIUS *and his* SOLDIERS *enter.*)

BRUTUS: Listen, he is here.
  March with nobility to meet him.

CASSIUS (*to his army*): Stand!
  (*To* BRUTUS) Most noble brother, you have done me
    wrong.

BRUTUS: Judge me, you gods! Do I wrong my enemies?
  And if not, how can I wrong a brother?

CASSIUS: Brutus, this show of yours hides wrongs,
  And when you do them—

BRUTUS: Cassius, enough.
  Keep it between us. I know you well.
  Let us not argue before our armies here.
  They should think there is only love between us.
  We'll talk in my tent. You may speak your anger,
  And I will listen.

CASSIUS: Pindarus, order our officers
  To lead their men away from here a little.

BRUTUS: Lucius, do the same, and let no man
  Come near our tent until our meeting's over.
  Let Lucilius and Titinius guard our door.

(*All but* BRUTUS *and* CASSIUS *exit.*)

Scene 3

Brutus's tent. The action continues from the last scene.

CASSIUS: I'll tell you how you've wronged me.
  You have publicly accused Lucius Pella
  Of taking bribes. I wrote you a letter
  Speaking for his side, because I know him,
  And you ignored it.

BRUTUS: You wronged yourself to write it.

CASSIUS: In such a time as this, it is not right
To notice every little fault.

BRUTUS: Let me tell you, Cassius, you yourself
Are often said to have an itching palm.[3]
It's said that, for gold, you give offices
To men who don't deserve them.

CASSIUS: I, an itching palm? If you weren't Brutus,
By the gods, that speech would be your last.

BRUTUS: Remember March, the ides of March?
Remember?
Did not great Julius bleed for justice's sake?
What villain stabbed his body for some reason
Other than for justice? Shall we now
Make our fingers dirty with bribes,
To sell our great honor for as much trash
As we can grab? I'd rather be a dog
Barking at the moon than such a Roman.

CASSIUS: Brutus, don't attack me. I won't stand it.
You forget yourself to try to give me orders.
I am a soldier, older in experience,
And more able than yourself to make decisions.

BRUTUS: Get out of here! You are not, Cassius.

CASSIUS: I am.

BRUTUS: I say you're not.

CASSIUS: Enough. Think of your health. Don't tempt me,
Or I'll forget myself.

BRUTUS: Away, small man.

CASSIUS: Is it possible?

---

3. have an itching palm be greedy for money

BRUTUS: Must I give way to your rash anger?
Shall I be frightened when a madman stares?

CASSIUS: Oh, you gods, must I stand for all this?

BRUTUS: All this and more, till your proud heart breaks.
Go show your slaves how fired up you are,
And make them tremble. I will not bow down
Before your angry temper. By the gods,
You'll swallow down the poison of your anger
Even if it splits you. From this day on,
I'll use your wasp-like temper for my laughter.

CASSIUS: Has it come to this?

BRUTUS: You say you are a better soldier. Prove it.
Make your bragging true, and it shall please me.
I would be glad to learn that you are noble.

CASSIUS: You wrong me, Brutus, you wrong me every
way.
I said an older soldier, not a better.
Did I say "better"?

BRUTUS: I don't care if you did.

CASSIUS: When Caesar lived, he dared not anger me so.

BRUTUS: Enough, enough! You dared not tempt him so.

CASSIUS: Do not presume so much upon my love.
I may do something I'll be sorry for.

BRUTUS: You've done something you should be sorry for.
I feel no terror, Cassius, at your threats.
For I am armed so strongly with my honor,
That they pass by me like the idle wind.
I sent a messenger to you to ask for gold,
And you denied me. I can raise no money
By dirty means. I'd rather squeeze money
From my heart and blood than take it by force

From the hands of peasants. I sent to you
For gold to pay my soldiers, which you denied me.
Was that done like Cassius?
Would I have answered Caius Cassius so?
When Marcus Brutus has become so greedy
To lock away such trash from his good friends,
Be ready, gods, with all your thunderbolts,
To dash him to pieces!

CASSIUS: I did not deny you.

BRUTUS: You did.

CASSIUS: I did not. A fool messenger brought back
The wrong answer. Brutus has split my heart.
A friend accepts a friend's faults, but you make
Mine greater than they are. You love me not.

BRUTUS: I do not like your faults.

CASSIUS: A friendly eye would never see such faults.

BRUTUS: A flatterer would not, even if they were
Huge as a mountain.

CASSIUS: Come, Antony, and young Octavius, come!
Revenge yourselves on Cassius alone.
For Cassius is tired of the world,
Threatened by one he loves like a brother,
Scolded like a slave, all his faults listed
To throw back in my face. Oh, I could weep
My spirit from my eyes! There is my dagger,

(*He offers his knife to* BRUTUS.)

And here my naked chest, my heart inside.
If you are a Roman, take it from me.
I who denied you gold will give my heart.
Strike as you did at Caesar. I know that
When you hated him worst, you loved him better

Than you ever loved Cassius.

BRUTUS: Put away your dagger.
    Be angry when you want; I'll let it pass.
    I'll take your insults as a passing mood.
    You carry anger as a flint[4] bears fire.
    When struck hard, you show a quick, bright spark,
    And then are cold again.

CASSIUS: Has Cassius lived to be no more than laughter
    To his Brutus, when his temper makes him angry?

BRUTUS: When I said that, I was bad-tempered too.

CASSIUS: Do you admit it? Give me your hand.

BRUTUS: And my heart too. (*They shake hands.*)

CASSIUS: Oh, Brutus!

BRUTUS: What's the matter?

CASSIUS: Don't you have enough love to bear with me
    When that bad temper which my mother gave me
    Makes me forget?

BRUTUS: Yes, Cassius, and from now on,
    When you are over-earnest with your Brutus,
    He'll think that it's your mother scolding him,
    And let you be.

(*A* POET *enters, followed by* LUCILLIUS, TITINIUS, *and*
LUCIUS.)

POET: Let me go in to see the generals.
    There is some grudge between them; it is not good
    For them to be alone.

LUCILIUS: You shall not bother them.

---

4. **flint** hard stone that makes a spark when struck by steel

POET: Nothing but death will stop me.

CASSIUS: What's going on? What's the matter?

POET: For shame, you generals, what do you mean?
　　Love and be friends, as two such men should do,
　　For I am sure I've seen more years than you.

CASSIUS: Ha, ha, how badly does this fellow rhyme!

BRUTUS: Get out of here, you foolish nobody!
　　You rascal, out!

CASSIUS: Away, away, be gone!

(*The* POET *exits.*)

BRUTUS: Lucilius and Titinius, tell the officers
　　To have their men bed down here for the night.

CASSIUS: And come yourselves to us immediately,
　　And bring Messala.

(LUCILIUS *and* TITINIUS *exit.*)

BRUTUS: Lucius, a bowl of wine.

(LUCIUS *exits.*)

CASSIUS: I did not think you could have been so angry.

BRUTUS: Oh, Cassius, I am sick with grief.

CASSIUS: It is not like you to give in to evils
　　Brought about by chance.

BRUTUS: No man bears sorrow better. Portia is dead.

CASSIUS: How's that? Portia?

BRUTUS: She is dead.

CASSIUS: How did I escape being killed just now
　　For what I said? Oh, what a terrible loss!
　　Of what sickness?

BRUTUS: Of missing me,
And of hearing that young Octavius
And Mark Antony have made themselves so strong.
That's what I'm told. They say she grew depressed
And, when her slaves were gone, ate burning coals.

CASSIUS: Oh, you ever-living gods!

(LUCIUS *enters with wine and candles.*)

BRUTUS: Speak no more of her. Give me a bowl of wine.
In this I bury all unkindness, Cassius.

(*He drinks.*)

CASSIUS: My heart is thirsty for that noble toast.
Fill, Lucius, till the wine overflows the cup.
I cannot drink too much of Brutus's love.

(*He drinks.* LUCIUS *exits.* TITINIUS *and* MESSALA *enter.*)

BRUTUS: Come in, Titinius. Welcome, good Messala.
Now, let's sit close around this candle here
And talk about what we need to do.

(*They sit.*)

Messala, I have received a letter
That young Octavius and Mark Antony
March on against us with a mighty army.
They seem to be heading for Philippi.

MESSALA: I have had letters with the same news.

BRUTUS: And anything else?

MESSALA: Yes. Octavius, Antony, and Lepidus
Have by proscription[5] put to death

---

5. proscription sentencing a man to death and seizing his
property

A hundred senators.

BRUTUS: Then our letters do not quite agree.
Mine speaks of seventy senators that died
By their proscription. Cicero was one.

CASSIUS: Cicero?

MESSALA: Cicero is dead,
And that by order of proscription.

BRUTUS: Well, let us then get on about the work
That faces those of us who are alive.
What do you think of marching to Philippi?

CASSIUS: I do not like it.

BRUTUS: Your reason?

CASSIUS: It is this:
It's better that the enemy seek us.
Let him waste his supplies, tire out his men,
Do himself harm. Meanwhile, we'll lie still,
And be well-rested, quick, alert, and strong.

BRUTUS: Good reasons must give way to better.
The people between here and Philippi
Are on our side only because of force.
They begrudge us the supplies we take from them.
When the enemy marches by, many will join them.
They'll be refreshed, larger, and confident.
We can cut them off from this advantage
If we march to Philippi and face them there,
With these people at our back.

CASSIUS: Hear me, good brother—

BRUTUS: Begging your pardon, Cassius, I'll go on.
You must also note that we've demanded
Everything from our friends that they could give.
Our force is at full strength. Our cause is ripe.

The enemy grows stronger every day.
We, at full strength, are ready to grow weaker.
There is a tide in the affairs of men
Which, taken at the flood, leads on to fortune.
If it's ignored, the voyage of their life
Is spent in shallow seas and misery.
We are now floating on that high tide,
And we must ride the current while we can
Or lose our chance.

CASSIUS: Then, as you wish, we'll march
And meet them at Philippi.

BRUTUS: The dark of night has fallen as we've talked,
And nature is demanding that we sleep.
We'll be stingy with her, and rest a little.
There is no more to say.

CASSIUS: No more. Good night.

(*They stand.*)

BRUTUS: We'll arise early and leave tomorrow.

BRUTUS: Lucius? (LUCIUS *enters.*) My gown.
(LUCIUS *exits.*) Good-bye, good Messala.
Good night, Titinius. Noble, noble Cassius,
Good night, and have good rest.

CASSIUS: Oh, my dear brother,
This night had such a bad beginning.
Let such division, Brutus, never come
Between our souls again.

(LUCIUS *enters with the gown.*)

BRUTUS: Everything is well.

CASSIUS: Good night, my lord.

BRUTUS: Good night, my brother.

TITINIUS *and* MESSALA: Good night, lord Brutus.

BRUTUS: Good night, everyone.

(*All but* BRUTUS *and* LUCIUS *exit.*)

Give me the gown. Where is your instrument?

LUCIUS (*yawning*): Here, in the tent.

BRUTUS: You speak sleepily. Poor boy,
I don't blame you. You've been awake too long.
Call Claudius and some other of my men.
I'll have them sleep on cushions in my tent.

LUCIUS: Varro and Claudius.

(VARRO *and* CLAUDIUS *enter.*)

VARRO: Calls my lord?

BRUTUS: I ask you, sirs, to sleep here in my tent.
It may be I shall wake you before morning
To tend to business with my brother Cassius.

VARRO: We will keep watch and wait for your commands.

BRUTUS: I will not have it so. Lie down, good sirs.

(*They lie down.*)

Look, Lucius, here's the book I asked you for.
I put it in the pocket of my robe.

LUCIUS: I was sure you did not give it to me.

BRUTUS: Bear with me, good lad. I forget too much.
Can you keep awake a little longer
And play a song or two upon your instrument?

LUCIUS: Yes, my lord, if it pleases you.

BRUTUS: It does, my boy.
I trouble you too much, but you are willing.

LUCIUS: It is my duty, sir.

BRUTUS: I would not urge your duty past your strength.
I know young bodies need a time of rest.

LUCIUS: I have already slept, my lord.

BRUTUS: It was well done, and you shall sleep again.
I will not keep you long. If I live,
I will be good to you.

(LUCIUS *plays and sings a song on his instrument and
falls asleep.*)

This is a sleepy tune. Oh, murderous sleep!
You lay your heavy club upon a boy
Who plays you music? Noble lad, good night.
I will not do you wrong by waking you.
If you nod, boy, you will break your instrument.
I'll take it from you and, good boy, good night.

(*He moves the instrument.*)

Let me see, let me see. Isn't the page turned down
Where I stopped reading? Hear it is, I think.

(*He reads.*)

How poorly this candle burns!

(*The* GHOST *of Caesar enters.*)

Who comes here?
I think it is the weakness of my eyes
That shapes this monstrous thing before me.
It's coming toward me—Are you any thing?
Are you some god, some angel, or some devil
That makes my blood cold and my hair stand up?
Tell me what you are.

GHOST: Your evil spirit, Brutus.

BRUTUS: Why do you come?

GHOST: To tell you, you shall see me at Philippi.

BRUTUS: Well, then I shall see you again?

GHOST: Yes, at Philippi.

BRUTUS: Why, I will see you at Philippi, then.

(*The* GHOST *exits.*)

> Now that I've found my courage, you disappear.
> Bad spirit, I would talk further with you—
> Boy, Lucius!—Varro, Claudius, sirs, wake up!

LUCIUS: The strings, my lord, are out of tune.

BRUTUS: He thinks he is still playing his instrument.
Lucius, wake up!

LUCIUS: My lord?

BRUTUS: Were you dreaming? Was that why you cried
out?

LUCIUS: My lord, I do not know that I cried out.

BRUTUS: Yes, you did. Did you see anything?

LUCIUS: Nothing, my lord.

BRUTUS: Go back to sleep, Lucius. You, Claudius!
(*To* VARRO) You there, wake up!

VARRO: My Lord?

CLAUDIUS: My Lord?

BRUTUS: Why did you cry out, sirs, in your sleep?

BOTH: Did we, my lord?

BRUTUS: Yes. Did you see anything?

VARRO: No, my lord, I saw nothing.

CLAUDIUS: Nor I, my lord.

BRUTUS: Go bring this message to my brother, Cassius.
Have him lead his forces off early this morning,
And we will follow.

BOTH: It shall be done, my lord.

(*They exit.*)

Act 5

Scene 1

Near Philippi. ANTONY, OCTAVIUS, *and their army enter.*

OCTAVIUS: Now, Antony, our hopes are not answered.
   You said the enemy would not come down,
   But would keep to the hills. It proves not so.
   Their armies are nearby. They mean to fight us
   Here at Philippi.

ANTONY: Don't worry. I know their secrets, and I know
   Why they have come. They could be most happy
   If they were someplace else. They want to scare us
   With this brave show, but I know better.

(*A* MESSENGER *enters.*)

MESSENGER: Be ready, generals.
   The enemy is coming on full force,
   And something must be done at once.

ANTONY: Octavius, lead your army slowly on
   To the left side of that flat field.

OCTAVIUS: No; I'll take the right side, you the left.

ANTONY: Who do you oppose me at this key moment?

OCTAVIUS: I do not oppose you, but I will do so.[1]

(*The sound of a drum.* BRUTUS, CASSIUS, *and their army
enter, including* LUCILIUS, TITINIUS, *and* MESSALA.)

BRUTUS: They've stopped. They want to talk.

---

1. **I will do so** Octavius and Antony later became enemies.
   After defeating Antony, Octavius became the first Roman
   Emperor.

80

CASSIUS: Stand fast, Titinius.

OCTAVIUS: Mark Antony, shall we begin the fighting?

ANTONY: No, we will wait for their attack.
Step forward. The generals want to talk.

(The leaders step toward each other.)

BRUTUS: Words before blows; is that it, countrymen?

OCTAVIUS: Not that we love words better, as you do.

BRUTUS: Good words are better than bad strokes,
Octavius.

ANTONY: In your bad strokes, Brutus, are good words.
I mean the hole you made in Caesar's heart,
Crying "Long live Caesar!"

BRUTUS: I do not know what kind of blows you'll give.
As for your words, at Caesar's funeral
They stole the honey from the Hybla[2] bees.
You also stole their buzzing, Antony,
And very wisely threaten before you sting.

ANTONY: As you did not, you villains, when your blades
Hacked one another in great Caesar's sides.
You showed your teeth like apes and crawled like dogs,
And bowed like slaves, kissing Caesar's feet,
While Casca struck him in the back! You flatterers!

CASSIUS: Flatterers? Now, Brutus, blame yourself.
This tongue would not be offending so today
If Cassius had had his way.

OCTAVIUS: Get to the point. If arguing makes us sweat,
The test of it will turn to redder drops.
Look, I draw a sword against conspirators.

---

2. Hybla A place in Sicily famous for producing honey

(He draws his sword.)

This sword shall not be sheathed again until
Great Caesar's wounds have been avenged, or till
Another Caesar[3] dies by traitors' swords.

BRUTUS: Caesar, you cannot die by traitors' hands
Unless you brought them with you.

OCTAVIUS: So I hope.
I was not born to die on Brutus's sword.

BRUTUS: If you were the noblest of your family,
You could not find a more honorable death.

OCTAVIUS: Come, Antony, away. Traitors, we throw
Defiance in your face. If you dare fight,
Come at us in the field.

(OCTAVIUS, ANTONY, and their army exit.)

CASSIUS: The storm is up, and everything is at stake.

BRUTUS: Lucilius, listen. A word with you.

(LUCILIUS and MESSALA step forward.)

LUCILIUS: My Lord?

(BRUTUS and LUCILIUS step aside together.)

MESSALA: What does my general say?

CASSIUS: This is my birthday, Messala.
On this very day was Cassius born.
Give me your hand. Be my witness, Messala,
That I am forced against my will to risk
All our liberties on this one battle.
You know, I have never believed in omens.

---

3. Another Caesar Octavius, Julius's adopted son, is referring
to himself.

Now I've changed my mind. Coming from Sardis,
Two eagles perched upon our battle flag.
Feeding from our soldiers' hands, they came
All the way to Philippi with us.
This morning they are gone. They've flown away,
And in their place come birds that eat the dead,
Flying over us and looking down at us.
Their shadows seem to be a cover
Under which we lie, ready for death.

MESSALA: Do not believe this.

CASSIUS: I believe it partly,
    For my spirit is ready for what comes,
    And I will meet all dangers without fear.

BRUTUS: Even so, Lucilius. (*He returns to* CASSIUS.)

CASSIUS: Now, most noble Brutus,
    May the gods stand friendly today, that we may
    Live to old age, forever friends in peace.
    But as this world always remains uncertain,
    Let's think about the worst thing that may happen.
    If we lose, this is the very last time
    That we shall speak together. What will you do?

BRUTUS: I always blamed Cato for the death
    Which he did give himself. I don't know why,
    But I do find it cowardly and vile
    To stop one's life for fear of what might happen.
    I would rather arm myself with patience
    And wait for what the gods above will do.

CASSIUS: Then, if we lose this fight, you are content
    To be led in triumph through the streets of Rome?

BRUTUS: No, Cassius, no. Do not think that Brutus
    Will ever go to Rome in chains. But here
    Must end the work begun on the ides of March.

I don't know whether we shall meet again.
Therefore, good-bye forever, Cassius.
If we do meet again, why, we shall smile.
If not, why then this parting was well-made.

CASSIUS: Forever and forever good-bye, Brutus.
If we do meet again, we'll smile indeed.
If not, it's true this parting was well-made.

BRUTUS: Why, then, lead on. Oh, that a man might know
The end of the day's work before it happens!
But it's enough to know this day will end,
And then the end is known. Come on, let's go!

(*They exit.*)

Scene 2

The battlefield. Trumpets. BRUTUS AND MESSALA *enter.*

BRUTUS: Ride, ride, Messala, and give these orders
To all the forces on the other side.

(*He hands* MESSALA *papers. Loud trumpets.*)

Let them attack at once, because I think
Octavius's wing now shows a lack of spirit,
And a sudden push may throw them over.
Ride, ride, Messala! Let them all come down.

(*They exit.*)

Scene 3

A hill near the battlefield. Trumpets. CASSIUS (*with a flag*) *and* TITINIUS *enter.*

CASSIUS: Look, Titinius, how the villains fly!
I have turned enemy to my own men.

I caught my flag-bearer running away;
I killed the coward and took it from him.

TITINIUS: Oh, Cassius, Brutus gave the word too soon.
He had the advantage on Octavius
But was too eager. His soldiers started looting,
And now Antony's men have us surrounded.

(PINDARUS *enters.*)

PINDARUS: Get away from here, my lord, away!
Mark Antony is in your tents, my lord.
Fly, noble Cassius, fly far away.

CASSIUS: This hill is far enough.—Look, Titinius,
Are those our tents that I see burning there?

TITINIUS: They are, my lord.

CASSIUS: Titinius, if you love me,
Get on my horse and bury your spurs in him
Until he's brought you up to those men there.
Then hurry back, and tell me whether they
Are friend or enemy.

TITINIUS: I will be back as quickly as a thought.

(*He exits.*)

CASSIUS: Go, Pindarus, get higher on that hill.
My sight was always weak. Watch Titinius,
And tell me what you see around the field.

(PINDARUS *goes up.*)

I was born this day. Time has come around,
And where I did begin, there shall I end.
My life has run its course. Tell me, what news?

PINDARUS (*calling from above*): Oh, my lord!
Titinius is circled all around

By horsemen that do press him to ride faster.
Now they are almost on him. Now, Titinius!
Now some are off their horses. Oh, he is too.
He's captured! (*Shouting is heard.*) Now they shout
  for joy.

CASSIUS: Come down. Look no more.
  Oh, coward that I am to live so long
  To see my best friend captured.

(PINDARUS *comes down.*)

  In Persia did I take you prisoner,
  And when I spared your life, I made you swear
  That whatever I did tell you, you would do.
  Come now, keep your promise. You are now free.
  With this sword that ran through Caesar's belly,
  Seek out my heart. Do not say anything.
  Here, take it now, and when my face is covered,
  Guide in the sword. (PINDARUS *stabs him.*)
  Caesar, you are revenged,
  Even with the sword that killed you.

(CASSIUS *dies.*)

PINDARUS: So I am free, yet I would not have been
  If I'd done what I wished.—Oh, Cassius!—
  Far from this country Pindarus will run,
  Where no Roman ever shall take note of him.

(*He exits.* TITINIUS *and* MESSALA *enter.*)

MESSALA: It's even, Titinius, because Octavius
  Is overthrown by noble Brutus's army,
  And Cassius's forces are beaten by Antony.

TITINIUS: This news will comfort Cassius.

MESSALA: Where did you leave him?

TITINIUS: On this hill with Pindarus, his slave.

MESSALA: Is not that he who lies upon the ground?

TITINIUS: This was he. Oh, my heart, Messala!
Cassius is no more. Oh, setting sun!
As in your red rays you do sink to night,
So in his red blood Cassius's day is set.
The sun of Rome is set. Our day is gone,
And cloudy dangers come. Our deeds are done.
My fear that we had lost has done this deed.
Pindarus! Where are you, Pindarus?

MESSALA: Seek him, Titinius, while I go to meet
The noble Brutus, thrusting this report
Into his ears. I may say "thrusting,"
For piercing swords and arrows tipped with poison
Shall be as welcome to the ears of Brutus
As news of this sad sight.

TITINIUS: Hurry, Messala,
And I will look around for Pindarus.

(MESSALA *exits.*)

Why did you send me forth, brave Cassius?
Did I not meet your friends, and did they not
Put on my head this wreath of victory[4]
To have me bring it to you? Didn't you hear them
shout?
Ah, you have misunderstood everything.

(*He lays the wreath on* CASSIUS'S *head.*)

---

4. **wreath of victory** Roman officers wore a crown of laurel
leaves as a sign of victory.

So Brutus had me do, and I have done it.
Brutus, come soon, and see what I have done.
By your permission, gods, I'll do a Roman's part.
Come, Cassius's sword, and find Titinius's heart!

(*He kills himself with Cassius's sword. Trumpets sound.*
BRUTUS, MESSALA, *young* CATO, STRATO, VOLUMNIUS,
LUCILIUS, *and other* OFFICERS *enter.*)

BRUTUS: Where, where, Messala, does his body lie?

MESSALA: Over there, and Titinius is mourning it.

BRUTUS: Titinius's face is upward.

CATO: He is killed.

BRUTUS: Oh, Julius Caesar, you are mighty yet.
Your spirit walks about and turns our swords
Into our own bodies. (*Low trumpets sound.*)

CATO: Brave Titinius!—
See how he has crowned dead Cassius.

BRUTUS: Are there two Romans such as these still living?
Good-bye, last of all the Romans.
It is impossible that Rome should ever
Breed your equal. Friends, I owe more tears
To this dead man than you shall see me pay.
I shall find time, Cassius; I shall find time.
Come, Lucilius, and come, young Cato.
Let us go back and set our soldiers on.
It's three o'clock, and, Romans, before night,
We'll try our courage in a second fight.

(*They exit.*)

88

Scene 4

The battlefield. BRUTUS, MESSALA, *young* CATO, LUCILIUS, *and* FLAVIUS *enter.*

BRUTUS: Yet, countrymen, oh, yet hold up your heads!

(BRUTUS, MESSALA, *and* FLAVIUS *exit.*)

CATO: What low thing does not? Who will go with me?
    I will proclaim my name around the field.
    I am the son of Marcus Cato! Here!
    An enemy to tyrants, and Rome's friend.

(*Antony's* SOLDIERS *enter and fight.*)

LUCILIUS: And I am Brutus, Marcus Brutus! I!
    Brutus, my country's friend! Know I am Brutus!

(*Young* CATO *is killed.*)

    Oh, young and noble Cato, are you down?
    Why, now you die as bravely as Titinius,
    And will be honored, being Cato's son.

SOLDIER (*seizing* LUCILIUS): Yield, or you die.

LUCILIUS: I yield only to die. (*Offering money*)
    There is so much here; kill me straight away.
    Kill Brutus, and be honored in his death.

SOLDIER: We must not. A noble prisoner!

(ANTONY *enters.*)

    Here comes the general. I'll tell the news—
    Brutus is taken. Brutus is taken, lord.

ANTONY: Where is he?

LUCILIUS: Safe, Antony. Brutus is safe enough.
    I dare assure you that no enemy

Shall ever take the noble Brutus alive.
The gods defend him from so great a shame!
When you find him, be he alive or dead,
He will be found like Brutus, like himself.

ANTONY: This is not Brutus, friend, but I assure you,
A prize no less in worth. Keep this man safe.
Give him all kindness. I would rather have
Such men as friends than enemies. Go on,
And see if Brutus is alive or dead.
Then bring word to us in Octavius's tent.

(*They exit in different directions.*)

Scene 5

Another part of the battlefield. BRUTUS, DARDANUS,
CLITUS, STRATO, *and* VOLUMNIUS *enter.*

BRUTUS: Come, poor remains of friends, rest on this rock.

(*He sits down.*)

CLITUS: Statilius showed the signal, but, my lord,
He did not come back. He's captured or killed.

BRUTUS: Sit down, Clitus. Killing is the word.
It is in fashion here. Listen, Clitus.

(*He whispers to* CLITUS.)

CLITUS: What, I, my lord? Not for all the world.
I'd rather kill myself.

BRUTUS: Peace, then, no words. Listen, Dardanus.

(*He whispers to* DARDANUS.)

DARDANUS: Shall I do such a deed? Oh, Clitus!

CLITUS: Oh, Dardanus! (*They step aside.*)
What bad favor did Brutus ask of you?

90

DARDANUS: To kill him, Clitus. Look, he meditates.[5]

BRUTUS: Come here, good Volumnius. A word with you.

VOLUMNIUS: What does my lord say?

BRUTUS: This, Volumnius:
  The ghost of Caesar has twice appeared to me:
  At Sardis, and last night here at Philippi.
  I know my hour has come. (*Low trumpets sound.*)

VOLUMNIUS: Not so, my Lord.

BRUTUS: No, I'm sure it has, Volumnius.
  You see the world and how it goes. Our enemies
  Have driven us to the edge of the pit.
  It is more worthy to jump in ourselves
  Than wait until they push us. Good Volumnius,
  Hold my sword while I run upon it.

VOLUMNIUS: That's not a job to give a friend, my lord.

(*Trumpets grow louder.*)

CLITUS: Run, run, my lord. This is no place to stay.

BRUTUS: Good-bye to you—to you, to all of you.
  My countrymen, my heart is glad that all my life
  I knew so many who were true to me.
  I have more glory on this losing day
  Than Antony and Octavius shall have in conquest.
  So good-bye all at once, for Brutus's tongue
  Has almost ended his life's history.
  Night hangs upon my eyes; my bones want rest.
  They have worked only to reach this hour.

(*Trumpets sound. Shouts offstage: "Fly, fly, fly!"*)

CLITUS: Fly, my lord, fly!

---

5. meditates thinks deeply and quietly

BRUTUS: Go. I will follow.

(*All exit but* BRUTUS *and* STRATO.)

> I ask you, Strato, stay here by your lord.
> You are a fellow worthy of respect.
> Hold my sword, and turn away your face
> While I run upon it. Will you, Strato?

STRATO: Give me your hand first. Good-bye, my lord.

BRUTUS: Good-bye, good Strato.

(*He runs on his sword.*)

> Caesar, now be still.
> I killed you with not half so good a will.

(BRUTUS *dies. Trumpets sound.* ANTONY *and* OCTAVIUS
enter with MESSALA, LUCILIUS, *and the army.*)

OCTAVIUS: What man is that?

MESSALA: My master's man. Strato, where is your master?

STRATO: Free from the slavery you are in, Messala.
> The conquerors can only make a fire of him.
> For Brutus alone has conquered himself,
> And no one else has honor by his death.

LUCILIUS: So it should be. I thank you, Brutus,
> For proving true what Lucilius said.

OCTAVIUS: I will accept all who served Brutus
> Into my service. Fellow, will you join me?

STRATO: Yes, if Messala recommends me to you.

OCTAVIUS: Do so, good Messala.

MESSALA: How did my master die?

STRATO: I held the sword, and he did run on it.

MESSALA: Octavius, then take him to follow you.
He did the last service to my master.

ANTONY: This was the noblest Roman of them all.
All the conspirators, except for him
Did what they did in envy of great Caesar.
He alone joined for what he thought was right.
His life was gentle, and the elements
So mixed in him that nature might stand up
And say to all the world, "This was a man."

OCTAVIUS: According to his honor, we respect him.
His bones shall lie inside my tent tonight,
Treated with honor, most like a soldier.
Call the army to rest, and let's away,
To share the glories of this happy day.

(*All exit.*)

SUMMARY OF PLAY

ACT 1

Julius Caesar has won total power in Rome. Caesar is well liked by the common people, but many noble Romans hate him. They are proud of being free citizens and fear that Caesar might make himself king. A soothsayer warns Caesar to "Beware the ides (the 15th) of March." Caesar and his loyal follower, Mark Antony, dismiss this warning.

Caius Cassius leads a group of nobles in a conspiracy to murder Caesar. Cassius knows that if their plan is to work, they need Caesar's friend, Marcus Brutus, to join the conspiracy. He thinks he can win Brutus over by appealing to his sense of honor.

ACT 2

The conspirators visit Brutus's house at night. Cassius convinces Brutus that Caesar is a threat to Rome's freedom. Brutus has doubts, but he agrees to join them. Cassius wants Mark Antony killed too, but Brutus talks him out of it. Brutus's wife, Portia, knows that something is troubling him.

It is now March 15. Caesar's wife, Calpurnia, fears for his safety and does not want him to go to the senate. He agrees to stay home. But one of the conspirators tells him that the senate wants to name him king that day. Caesar changes his mind and leaves with them.

ACT 3

The conspirators gather around Caesar and stab him to death. Antony tells Brutus that he will follow him as he followed Caesar. Brutus lets Antony speak at Caesar's funeral. But Antony is only pretending to support Brutus. He uses his speech to turn the people against the conspirators. Word comes that Octavius, Caesar's adopted son, is near Rome with his army. Brutus and Cassius are forced to run for their lives.

ACT 4

Antony and Octavius are the new rulers of Rome. They mean to kill anyone who may oppose them. Meanwhile, Brutus and Cassius argue with each other. Each thinks the other has wronged him. They argue bitterly, but then they make up. They plan to march their army to the town of Philippi. There they will make their stand against Octavius and Antony. Caesar's ghost visits Brutus in his tent. He warns Brutus that he will see him again at Philippi.

ACT 5

At Philippi, the enemy leaders exchange insults before they fight. The first battle results in a stand-off. Antony defeats Cassius; Brutus defeats Octavius. But Cassius, thinking that he and Brutus have lost, kills himself. Brutus throws his troops into a second battle. This time they are thoroughly beaten. Brutus has one of his officers help him kill himself. Antony, coming upon his enemy's body, calls Brutus "the noblest Roman of them all."

REVIEWING YOUR READING

ACT 1

FINDING THE MAIN IDEA

1. Cassius says he wants Caesar killed because

    (A) he wants revenge for Pompey's defeat   (B) he thinks Caesar is too weak to rule   (C) he hates the thought that one man should rule Rome   (D) he wants to rule Rome himself.

REMEMBERING DETAILS

2. Caesar wants Antony to touch Calpurnia during the Lupercal race because, according to old tales,

    (A) it will help Antony win the race   (B) it will make Calpurnia able to have a child   (C) it will give Antony the power to tell the future   (D) it will help Caesar become king.

3. Casca speaks of all these "wonders" taking place, except

    (A) a lion in the streets   (B) an owl appearing at noon
    (C) a slave whose hand was on fire but was not harmed
    (D) burning men flying through the air.

DRAWING CONCLUSIONS

4. Casca implies that Caesar looked sad as he returned from the race because

    (A) he fainted   (B) he didn't understand Cicero's speech
    (C) he really wanted to take the crown   (D) he cared little for the "low people."

5. Cassius wants Brutus to be part of the conspiracy because

    (A) Brutus is respected in a way he and the others are not
    (B) Caesar trusts Brutus, but he does not trust Cassius
    (C) Brutus is a good man in a fight   (D) Both A and B are true.

USING YOUR REASON

6. Noble Romans hate the thought of Caesar becoming king because

    (A) they are free and equal, and Caesar is no better than any of them   (B) Caesar is one of the common people and not worthy of being a king   (C) Caesar will lead the Romans into wars they cannot win   (D) Both A and B are true.

7. From what happens in the first act, you can predict that
    (A) Brutus probably will not join in the plot to kill Caesar
    (B) Antony probably will be brought into the plot to kill Caesar
    (C) Caesar will be killed on the ides of March   (D) Cassius will
    back out of the plot at the last minute.

THINKING IT OVER

8. Shakespeare has already shown us a great deal about his
    characters. Write a sentence describing the kind of person each of
    the following characters is: Caesar, Brutus, Cassius, and Casca.

ACT 2

FINDING THE MAIN IDEA

1. The main point of Scene 1 is that
    (A) Brutus has trouble sleeping at night   (B) Brutus loves Portia
    very much   (C) Brutus joins the plot to kill Caesar, but he has
    serious doubts   (D) Portia wants to know Brutus's secrets.

2. The main point of Scene 2 is that
    (A) Caesar is persuaded to go to the Capitol   (B) Caesar is a
    brave man   (C) Caesar does not share Calpurnia's superstitions
    (D) Brutus is among the men who come to Caesar's house.

REMEMBERING DETAILS

3. Who is the last man brought into the conspiracy?
    (A) Brutus   (B) Decius   (C) Metellus   (D) Caius Ligarius

DRAWING CONCLUSIONS

4. Which of these characters knows who is involved in the
    conspiracy?
    (A) Antony   (B) Artemidorus   (C) the Soothsayer   (D) Lucius

5. Which of these statements is most likely true?
    (A) Brutus knows that the letter thrown through his window is a
    fake.   (B) Caesar does not believe in augurers.   (C) Brutus
    himself wants to be a king.   (D) By the end of Act 2, Brutus has
    told Portia about the conspiracy.

USING YOUR REASON

6. An *anachronism* (uh-NAK-ro-nihz-um) is a mistake in placing
   people, places, or events in time. For example, having ancient
   Romans driving cars would be an anachronism. What
   anachronism occurs in this act?

   (A) a gun being fired   (B) a person trying to interpret dreams
   (C) a Roman woman demanding that her husband tell her his
   secrets   (D) a clock striking

7. From what has happened in the first two acts, you can predict that
   (A) Portia will warn Caesar about the conspiracy   (B) Caesar will
   pay attention to the soothsayer's warning   (C) Caesar will go to
   the Capitol and be killed there   (D) Antony will join the
   conspiracy.

THINKING IT OVER

8. How would you contrast Portia and Calpurnia?

ACT 3

FINDING THE MAIN IDEA

1. The main thing that happens after Caesar's murder is that
   (A) Brutus proves himself to be a man of honor   (B) Antony
   turns the people against the conspirators   (C) Octavius comes to
   Rome   (D) Cinna the poet is killed.

REMEMBERING DETAILS

2. To what does Caesar compare himself in explaining why he will
   not change his mind?

   (A) fire   (B) a dog   (C) the sky   (D) the North Star

3. Who is the last man to stab Caesar?

   (A) Brutus   (B) Cassius   (C) Casca   (D) Cinna

4. What does Caesar leave to the people of Rome in his will?

   (A) money   (B) land for parks   (C) his house   (D) both A and B

DRAWING CONCLUSIONS

5. We can conclude that Antony

   (A) was secretly glad that Caesar was killed   (B) was willing to share power with Brutus and Cassius   (C) was too shrewd to stand up to Brutus and Cassius after Caesar's death   (D) was too broken up by Caesar's death to stand up to Brutus and Cassius.

6. One point that Shakespeare is trying to make in Act 3, Scene 2, is
    (A) people's minds can easily be turned by smooth speech
    (B) Antony is a liar, while Brutus is honest   (C) Brutus is more popular with the common people than Caesar was
    (D) both A and B.

USING YOUR REASON

7. From what has happened in this act, you can predict that
    (A) the conspirators will "get away with murder"   (B) the conspirators will all be caught and punished   (C) Antony will take Caesar's place   (D) Antony and Octavius will be allies.

THINKING IT OVER

8. In his funeral speech, Mark Antony says several times that "Brutus is an honorable man." In what ways does Brutus's honor lead him into danger?

ACT 4

FINDING THE MAIN IDEA

1. The most important thing we learn in this act is that
    (A) Antony and Octavius are killing anyone who might oppose them   (B) Brutus and Cassius are fighting with each other
    (C) Brutus and Cassius will battle Antony and Octavius for control of Rome   (D) Brutus is troubled by visions of Caesar's ghost.

REMEMBERING DETAILS

2. Antony and Octavius agree to share power with Lepidus because
    (A) he is rich, and his money will be useful to them   (B) he will bear some of the blame for the killing they are doing   (C) he is a tough soldier but easily controlled   (D) both B and C.

3. Pindarus is
    (A) one of Brutus's officers   (B) Antony's slave   (C) one of Cassius's officers   (D) Cassius's slave.

100

4. Brutus accuses Cassius of

(A) taking bribes   (B) conspiring with Antony against him
(C) being a poor soldier   (D) being a coward.

DRAWING CONCLUSIONS

5. Which of these beliefs expressed by a character earlier in the play
has proven to be true?

(A) Antony's belief that Cassius is not dangerous   (B) Brutus's
belief that Antony is not dangerous   (C) Antony's belief that
Caesar's murder will lead to civil war   (D) Brutus's belief that
killing Caesar will save the Republic

6. Which of the following statements has *not* proven to be true?

(A) Antony is concerned with carrying out Caesar's wishes.
(B) Portia is willing to take her own life.   (C) It is easy for
people to persuade Brutus to do what they want him to do.
(D) Cassius easily loses his temper and acts rashly.

USING YOUR REASON

7. From what has happened in this act, you can predict that

(A) Cassius will betray Brutus   (B) Brutus will, somehow,
eventually pay for betraying Caesar   (C) Brutus and Antony will
agree to share power and there will be no battle   (D) Caesar's
ghost will cause Brutus's courage to fail.

THINKING IT OVER

8. The ghost tells Brutus, "I am your evil spirit," not "I am Caesar's
ghost." What do you think Shakespeare meant by this?

ACT 5

FINDING THE MAIN IDEA

1. A good "headline" for the last act might be

(A) "Rome Is Saved from Tyranny"   (B) "Brutus and Cassius Die
Bravely in Battle"   (C) "Brutus Dies Because of Cassius's
Mistakes"   (D) "Brutus Loses Everything but Is Honored by His
Enemies."

REMEMBERING DETAILS

2. Before the battle, the enemy commanders
   (A) exchange news from Rome   (B) exchange insults   (C) fire
   arrows at one another   (D) will not speak to one another.

3. Cassius kills himself because
   (A) Brutus is taken prisoner   (B) he thinks Titinius has been
   taken prisoner   (C) the battle has been lost   (D) he wants to die
   on his birthday.

4. Antony calls Brutus "the noblest Roman of them all" because
   (A) Brutus killed himself to avoid being captured   (B) Brutus
   fought bravely in the battle   (C) Brutus refused to take bribes
   (D) only Brutus joined the conspiracy because he thought Caesar
   was a danger to Romans' freedom, not for personal reasons.

DRAWING CONCLUSIONS

5. The main reason Brutus chooses to die rather than be captured by
   Antony is that
   (A) he doesn't want to have his property seized   (B) he doesn't
   want to be put on trial for killing Caesar   (C) he doesn't want to
   be led through the streets of Rome in Antony's victory parade
   (D) he doesn't want to live to see Antony rule Rome.

6. Lucilius identifies himself as Brutus because (A) he wants
   Antony's soldiers to stop looking for the real Brutus   (B) he
   wants to die   (C) he wants glory for himself   (D) he wants to be
   treated as a noble prisoner.

USING YOUR REASON

7. Shakespeare implies that Brutus and Cassius might have won if
   (A) Cassius had not been so sure things were hopeless   (B) they
   had not marched to Philippi   (C) Brutus had not been so
   honorable   (D) both B and C.

THINKING IT OVER

8. Who do you think is the "hero" of this play? Who do you think is
   the "villain"? Explain your reasons. (You may decide that the play
   has no hero or villain. If so, tell why you think so.)